Good Eating's
Entertain With Ease

by
Heather J. McPherson

The Orlando Sentinel

For my husband, Spencer Pettit,
who is truly the better half,
and my parents, Jean and Bob McPherson,
who encouraged all three of their children
to be gracious hosts.

A toast to the following people who made this book possible:

John Blexrud, Lita Geier and Cindy King of the Orlando Sentinel's Marketing department.

Steve Doyle, Mick Lochridge, Wendy Spirduso, Linda Shrieves Beatty, Susan Whigham and April Medina of the Sentinel's Newsfeatures department.

Art director Melissa Slimick Huerta, a great friend and colleague, who knew me years before I ever thought that dinner for 60 people in the back yard was a piece of cake.

Sentinel recipe testers Betty Boza and Phyllis Gray and former Sentinel food editor Dorothy Chapman.

Sentinel photographers Tom Burton, Roberto Gonzalez, Barbara V. Perez, Bobby Coker and Gary Bogdon. And especially Lee Fiedler for scanning in all the pictures.

Also, Karen Sullivan, Judy Wick, Jill Shargaa, Ann Williams and Kelly Dill for sharing recipes.

Polly Golden of the Florida Beef Council, Anita File of Lewis & Neale and Barbara Bingham of the Distilled Spirits Council. Also, Pyrex Portables, American Spice Trade Association, National Honey Board, Rice Council, California Olive Commission, California Walnut Committee, California Grape Commission and Artichoke Advisory Board, Le Creuset, Pier 1, Truffles and Trifles, Fitz & Floyd and Wood Stone & Steel.

And especially to Jake and Laurie Vest, Amy Sadowsky and Patrick Reilly, Peggy Gage and George Dunn, Marci and Allen Arthur, Cathy and Gary Kerns, Leslie and Michael Poole, Mary Grunwald, Fran Coker, Dixie Tate and Curt Fields for always being such great guests.

McPherson, Heather

Library of Congress Cataloging-in-Publication Data

McPherson, Heather J.
    Good eating's entertain with ease / by Heather McPherson.
        p.   cm.
    Includes index.
    ISBN 0-8092-2924-2
    1. Entertaining.   2. Cookery.   3. Quick and easy cookery.
    I. Title.
    TX731.M396   1997
    642'.4—dc21   97-24286
                                                                        CIP

Contents

Setting the Stage

Setting the stage

The oven buzzer goes off.

The kitchen permeates with the savory smell of the Peach Brandy Poundcake.

You remove the fragrant dessert from the Bundt pan and smile wryly as you see how beautiful the delicate lemon verbena leaves look baked into the top.

Take that, Martha, you say to yourself.

The cake cools completely, and then you read the final recipe instruction: *Place on a serving plate, and garnish the plate with lemon verbena sprigs and begonias.*

Serving plate? Fresh flowers?

You just know that Martha Stewart is snickering somewhere.

Selecting dinnerware

Don't panic, this is where the fun comes in. Selecting dinnerware offers an opportunity to be creative with platters, serving bowls and table settings.

First, there are no rules. Your very best dishware can pair nicely with interesting pieces from second-hand stores. These shops carry everything from funky salt and pepper shakers to glass antique dishware. Great finds include custom-cut lazy Susan pieces, McCoy pottery or versatile Depression glass.

Think of serving platters as functional canvases for special occasion food. They showcase your best culinary efforts: a regal crown roast at a Christmas dinner party, rosebud-adorned petit fours at a holiday cookie exchange or a selection of sushi at a New Year's Eve cocktail party.

Purchase versatile presentation dishes that will take you from season to season and can be used for informal as well as formal functions.

When shopping, visualize a platter on different table backgrounds (marble, plain cloth, wicker, etc.). Think about the foods you serve. Is the pattern suitable for antipasto? How about tartlets? A good purchase is not necessarily the platter that earns yes answers to all of your questions. However, the exercise will train you to look at houseware items for what they can be, not what the store display indicates they are.

Don't overlook garden shops for creative plates, platters and bowls. New clay pots and terra cotta draining trays can be used to serve all sorts of food. Plastic, faux stone pedestal pots make striking serving bowls for sangria and punch.

Open up the china cabinet and dust off a seldom used champagne bucket and use it as an elegant holder for biscuits at a holiday brunch. Clear pitchers of water can dress up a table when slices of lemon, orange and carambola (star fruit) are added. And a raised cake plate filled with cookies gives height and interest to any table.

Creating a look

French leaves and silver and gold doilies should be in every party planner's bag of tricks. Doilies add lacy elegance, and the French leaves (available at most gourmet stores) add a sophisticated, catered look.

Dress down platters or bowls with cotton napkins that feature whimsical motifs (fish, geometric shapes, etc.) or have a checkerboard or fleur-de-lis pattern. Cloth napkins or cut fabric used as a place mat under clear plain platters add dimension and mood to the table. Choose contrasting colors for maximum visual appeal.

Go from Christmas to Easter with the same platter by playing up the appropriate seasonal color in the plate's pattern. A platter painted with soft yellow, blue and green hues can go holly jolly with a few sprigs of rosemary and garnishes of whole cranberries. And yellow, one of Christmas-time's most underused colors, is a marvelous match for red and green. Yellow plays up the warm glow of candles and practically glistens in the reflection of tree lights.

The following spring, use the same platter for Easter fare, highlighting the pastel blue color. Tendrils of curling ribbon strewn throughout a selection of cookies or a sprig of mint with an assortment of seasonal fruits will offer a cool spring look and scent.

If mixing and matching dishware is not your forte, stick with the little black dress of platters: the demure white oval. Its classic, elongated shape is great for easy reaching on buffets, coffee tables and dinner tables. And its neutral color makes the shades and textures of fresh herbs and cut vegetables pop off the plate. You can snaz it up or take it down a notch in the same manner you would other platters. Ornaments artfully placed around a white platter, for example, take the plate from plain to all-dressed-up in seconds. At New Year's Eve, that same plain platter can sparkle when paired with star-studded cobalt stemware or gold napkins.

Don't overlook your menu for serving inspiration. Offer a sweet potato bisque in mini pumpkins for individual servings or use a large pumpkin as a tureen. Hollowed-out peasant bread used as bowls is another easy way to add dimension to a table.

Setting the table

Whether you set up a buffet or sit-down dinner depends on how many people you are entertaining.

If your table seats only six people, don't try to squeeze in eight. However, that doesn't mean you can't have a nice sit-down meal. If you have card or resin tables, consider turning your living room into a bistro setting. Covered with appropriate tablecloths, the tables will look fine. (Some rental companies have folding chair slipcovers if you really want to dress up the room.)

Buffets are best for large groups. When arranging the food, make sure the items flow. For example, sauces and condiments should be placed near the foods they enhance.

Keep an eye on the buffet table during the evening to replenish foods as needed. An easy way to do this is to have several bowls of the same dips, sauces, etc. When one is nearly empty, simply substitute the full bowl. This avoids scraping food at the table or spilling while trying to refill the bowls from huge containers.

Most people don't realize the versatility of serving options that they have on hand. Dust off dishware weeks before a party and spread the pieces over the dining room table. Unless you put them side-by-side, you may never know how well an heirloom platter works with a five-and-dime bowl.

20 20-minute Appetizers

Bubbalou's Bodacious Bar-B-Q's Texas Caviar

This Texas caviar can be made ahead
and stored in the refrigerator for two weeks.
Yield: 8 servings

2 (15.8-ounce) cans black-eyed peas
3/4 cup salad oil
1/2 cup red-wine vinegar
1/2 cup finely chopped celery
1/2 cup finely chopped red onion
1/3 teaspoon salt
1/3 teaspoon ground black pepper
2 to 3 cloves garlic, crushed
Liberal dash Tabasco

1. Drain and rinse black-eyed peas in cold water. Transfer to glass bowl.

2. In separate bowl, add balance of ingredients and whisk thoroughly. Pour over black-eyed peas and stir together gently.

3. Store in refrigerator until ready to serve.

Recipe note: This flavorful dip tastes great in 20 minutes, but when refrigerated
overnight or longer, the ingredients come to full flavor.)

Harvey's Bistro's Smoked Shrimp and Artichoke Spread

The well-stocked pantry will include the ingredients for this recipe.
A mixer transforms them into a wonderful smoky dish for crackers.
Yield: about 4 appetizer servings

1 (8-ounce) package cream cheese, softened
1/4 teaspoon Worcestershire sauce
1 tablespoon fresh lemon juice
Dash Tabasco sauce
2 teaspoons Spike All-Purpose
  Seasoning (available at health-food and
  some grocery stores)
1/8 teaspoon liquid smoke
1/4 (10-ounce) package frozen artichoke hearts,
  cooked and diced
1/4 pound (any size) shrimp, shelled, deveined,
  cooked and cut into medium dice
Toasted French baguette croutons or crackers

1. In electric mixer bowl or food processor container, place cream cheese and beat on medium speed until creamy. Add Worcestershire, lemon juice, Tabasco, Spike and liquid smoke.

2. Fold in diced artichoke hearts and shrimp.

3. Serve with toasted French baguette croutons or crackers.

Deli Roast Beef and Roasted Red Pepper Crostini

Convenience products such as bottled roasted red peppers and a packaged cheese blend
help create this fast and flavorful treat.
Yield: 36 appetizers

2 (8-ounce) loaves French bread
  (about 2 1/2 -inch diameter), cut into
  1/2 -inch thick slices
3 tablespoons garlic-flavored olive or
  vegetable oil
3/4 pound thinly sliced deli roast beef
12-ounce jar roasted red peppers, rinsed,
  drained and chopped
2 cups shredded Italian cheese blend

1. Heat oven to 450 F.

2. Lightly brush top side of each bread slice with oil; arrange on two baking sheets. Bake in a 450 F oven for 6 to 8 minutes or until light golden brown.

3. Layer equal amounts of beef, red pepper and cheese over toasted bread. Return to oven; bake an additional 2 to 4 minutes or until cheese is melted. Serve immediately.

Recipe note: Bread may be toasted ahead of time and stored in an airtight container.

Black Bean Salsa

This recipe first appeared in "The Florida Cookbook — A Lighter Look at Southern Cooking" by Charlotte Balcomb Lane. The concept is simple, but the flavors are complex and intriguing.
Yield: 12-14 servings

1 (15-ounce) can black beans, drained
1 (12-ounce) jar salsa
1/4 cup chopped fresh cilantro
1/4 teaspoon cumin
2 tablespoons freshly squeezed lime juice

1. In the work bowl of a food processor or blender, roughly chop the black beans, being careful not to puree them.

2. Stir in salsa, cilantro, cumin and lime juice.

Recipe note: You can serve this right away with tortilla chips. If stored in the refrigrator overnight, the flavors intensify even more.

Creamy Basil Dip

Serve with chilled tortellini, boiled shrimp, blanched asparagus or cooked artichoke leaves.
Yield: 1 1/4 cups

1/4 cup fresh lemon or lime juice
1 teaspoon sugar
1 cup chopped fresh basil leaves
1/8 to 1/4 teaspoon salt
2 cloves garlic, chopped
1 cup regular or fat-free mayonnaise
Basil leaf for garnish
Thin strips of lime or lemon rind for garnish

1. In the work bowl of a blender or food processor, combine all ingredients except garnishes. Pulse mixture by using the on-and-off button until well-blended. Be careful not to puree mixture.

2. Spoon into a serving bowl, cover and refrigerate. Garnish when ready to serve.

Cucumber Mint Raita

Raitas are cool condiments found in Indian cookery.
Serve with celery sticks, spicy chips or crisp bread sticks.
Yield: 1 1/2 cups

1 cup nonfat plain yogurt
3/4 cup peeled, seeded, diced cucumber
1 1/2 tablespoons shredded fresh mint
2 teaspoons honey
Pinch cumin, salt, ground red pepper,
   ground cinnamon, ground cloves

1. Stir ingredients in a medium bowl;
   adjust flavors to taste.

Recipe note: Keep dips cool on the buffet table by putting them in small bowls that sit inside larger bowls filled with ice chips. Mix and match the color of the bowls for a festive look.

Red Pepper Bruschetta With Feta

Tangy feta marries well with the robust flavor
of roasted red pepper in this recipe.
Yield: 18 slices

1 (7-ounce) jar roasted red peppers, drained
   and chopped
1 garlic clove, peeled and finely chopped
Olive oil
1 teaspoon lemon juice
1/4 cup finely chopped green onions
1 (4-ounce) package crumbled feta cheese
   or finely chopped feta cheese
1 loaf French bread, cut into
   1/2-inch-thick slices

1. Mix red peppers, garlic, 1 tablespoon olive oil, lemon juice, green onions and feta cheese; set aside.

2. Lightly brush bread slices with olive oil and place on a baking sheet. Broil on each side until lightly toasted.

3. Top each slice with about 1 tablespoon of pepper mixture.

Tapenade

*Serve tapenade as a relish, sandwich spread
or a dip with bread sticks or chips.
Yield: 1 cup*

3/4 cup pitted, chopped black olives
1 tablespoon fresh parsley
2 tablespoons finely grated carrots
2 tablespoons finely chopped green onion
Hot pepper sauce to taste
1 teaspoon minced garlic
1 tablespoon lemon juice
1/2 teaspoon Italian seasoning
1 teaspoon chopped cilantro
1 finely chopped plum tomato
1 teaspoon spicy mustard

1. Combine all ingredients in a bowl and mix well.

Recipe note: For a smooth texture, place all ingredients in the work bowl of a food processor or blender and pulse using the on-off switch, being careful not to puree the mixture.

Other spices that work well in this mix include curry powder and chili powder.

Bacon Cheddar Dip

*This is a great way to use leftover bacon.
This dip can be made up to 2 days in advance.
Yield: 1 3/4 cups*

1/4 cup finely chopped cooked bacon
1 cup sour cream
1/2 cup Cheddar cold pack cheese spread,
   softened
3 tablespoons chopped fresh parsley
1 green onion, chopped (including green tops)
Hot pepper sauce to taste

1. In a medium bowl, combine chopped bacon, sour cream and cheese spread until well-blended.

2. Stir in parsley, green onions and pepper sauce. Chill until ready to serve.

Feta Avocado Spread

Serve this spread with sliced baguette rounds.
Also it can be used as a tangy celery filling or sandwich spread.
Yield: 3 1/2 cups

1 (4-ounce) package feta cheese, crumbled
1 tablespoon olive oil
4 ripe avocados, peeled, seeded and cut
   into chunks
1/2 teaspoon hot sauce
Juice of 1 lemon
Salt to taste

1. In a medium bowl, combine all ingredients with a fork until well-blended. Mixture should be slightly lumpy.

2. Spoon into a serving bowl and refrigerate until ready to serve.

Recipe note: For an elegant presentation, spoon a small amount onto the large ends of endive leaves and arrange on a round platter.

Fenwick Catering's Hot Crab Meat Dip

This is one of the easiest and most enduring party appetizers.
This dip can be made up 2 days in advance, if desired.
Yield: 12 servings

1 pound Alaskan crab meat, coarsely chopped
1 pound cream cheese
1/2 cup mayonnaise
1 bunch green onions, top and bulbs
   finely chopped
2 dashes Tabasco sauce
1 teaspoon Lea & Perrin's Worcestershire Sauce
1/2 cup slivered almonds, toasted

1. Heat oven to 350 F.

2. Blend together all ingredients except nuts. Spoon into bake-and-serve dish. Sprinkle top with slivered almonds. Bake 20 minutes. Serve warm with choice of crackers, melba rounds or toast points.

Shrimp Quesadillas

Serve these happy-hour favorites with bowls of cool sour cream or salsa.
Substitute chopped, cooked chicken for the shrimp, if desired.
Yeild: 4 appetizer servings

1/2 cup ricotta cheese
2 green onions, sliced (including green tops)
Hot sauce to taste (optional)
4 (7-inch) flour tortillas
1/2 pound medium-size shrimp, cooked, peeled, deveined and chopped
1 small tomato, chopped
1/2 cup shredded Monterey Jack cheese

1. Heat oven to 450 F.

2. In a small bowl, combine ricotta cheese, onions and pepper sauce. Spread on 2 flour tortillas. Sprinkle with half of the cooked shrimp. Top with remaining tortillas.

3. Top tortillas with remaining shrimp, tomato and cheese. Bake 5-8 minutes or until cheese melts. Let rest for 5 minutes. Cut into wedges and serve.

Spicy White Bean Dip

Add this dip to your tailgate repertoire.
All the ingredients are items you probably have in the kitchen.
Yeild: 1 1/2 cups

1 (16-ounce) can cannellini (white kidney) beans, rinsed and drained
2 cloves garlic, chopped
1 tablespoon olive oil
2 teaspoons fresh lemon juice
Hot pepper sauce to taste (optional)
1/4 teaspoon seasoned salt
1/2 teaspoon cumin
1/4 cup finely chopped cilantro

1. Combine all ingredients in the work bowl of a food processor. Blend until smooth, being careful not to puree mixture.

2. Spoon into a serving bowl and refrigerate until ready to serve.

Recipe note: Serve with crisp vegetables or toasted pita bread triangles.

Spencer's Pesto Pizza

Prepared pizza shells, available at most supermarkets,
make quick work of this appetizer.
Yield: 20 servings

2 large prepared pizza shells
6 tablespoons pesto (see note)
1 (14-ounce) can artichoke hearts, drained and
   roughly chopped
2 cups finely shredded Parmesan cheese

1. Heat oven to 425 F.

2. Spread pesto evenly over each pizza shell. Top with equal amounts of chopped artichoke hearts. Cover both with 1 cup shredded Parmesan cheese.

3. Bake for 15 minutes, or until cheese is slightly golden and bubbly. Let rest on counter for 5 minutes. Cut into thin wedges and serve.

Recipe note: We prefer the Boboli brand shells for this recipe. Prepared basil and sun-dried tomato pesto is available in most supermarkets. These wedges make an excellent side dish for a pasta dinner.

Roasted Pepper Red Onion Bread

If dinner preparations are taking longer than expected,
a flavorful bread can ease eager appetites.
Yield: 8 servings

1 (14-inch) large loaf Italian or whole-wheat bread
1 red onion, peeled and sliced thin
3/4 cup sliced roasted red peppers
3 tablespoons olive oil
3 tablespoons grated Parmesan cheese
1/2 teaspoon salt
1/4 teaspoon ground black pepper

1. Heat oven to 400 F. Slice bread in half lengthwise.

2. Toss remaining ingredients in a bowl until the onion slices are separated. Cover both sections of the bread with an even layer of this mix.

3. Bake bread directly on the oven rack until crispy and the top is lightly browned, about 8 minutes. Remove the bread carefully and let stand a few minutes before slicing crosswise into 2-inch pieces.

Joe's Mustard Sauce for Shellfish

*In Miami Beach, you know stone crab season has begun
when the lines start forming at South Florida's most-famous seafood institution,
Joe's Stone Crab restaurant. And Mustard Sauce is the preferred dipping sauce for the shellfish.
But don't reserve it just for the stone crabs; serve it with other crab and shrimp as well.
Yield: 1 1/4 cups*

3 1/2 teaspoons Colman's dry mustard,
  or to taste
1 cup mayonnaise
2 tablespoons heavy cream
2 tablespoons milk
2 teaspoons Worcestershire sauce
1 teaspoon A-1 Steak Sauce
Pinch of salt

1. Put 3 teaspoons of the dry mustard in a mixing bowl. Add the mayonnaise and, using an electric mixer on low speed, beat for 1 minute.

2. Add the cream, milk, Worcestershire sauce, steak sauce and salt. Beat on low until creamy, about 2 minutes.

3. Add the remaining 1/2 teaspoon dry mustard or more to taste, if you desire a sauce with a little bite.

4. Transfer the sauce to a small glass bowl, cover with plastic wrap and refrigerate until ready to serve.

To get the real thing for this spicy sauce, call Francesca's Favorites at 1-800-865-2722 or write Joe's Stone Crab Restaurant, Take Away, 227 Biscayne St., Miami, Fla. 33139.

Lime Cream Fruit Dip

Because they are light and refreshing,
fruit appetizers are great for warm-weather gatherings.
Yield: 1 cup

1 (8-ounce) carton sour cream
1 to 2 tablespoons sugar
2 teaspoons grated lime peel
1 tablespoon fresh lime juice
Assorted fresh fruits (apples, bananas, grapes,
   strawberries, kiwifruit, melon)

1. In a small bowl, stir together all ingredients except fruit. Cover; refrigerate 15 minutes.

2. Serve with fresh fruit.

Recipe note: Orange peel and orange juice may be substituted for the lime peel and lime juice.

Sun-Dried Tomato Bruschetta With Basil

Keep a jar of marinated sun-dried tomatoes in the cupboard
to make appetizers for unexpected guests.
Yield: 18 slices

1 (8-ounce) jar marinated, sun-dried tomatoes,
   drain, reserving 2 tablespoons of the
   marinating oil
2 garlic cloves, minced
1/2 cup finely chopped fresh basil
1 loaf French bread, cut into 1/2 -inch-
   thick slices

1. Chop sun-dried tomatoes and combine with garlic and basil.

2. Lightly brush bread slices with reserved olive oil and place on a baking sheet. Broil on each side until lightly toasted.

3. Top each slice with about 1 tablespoon of sun-dried tomato mixture.

The king of crab

Alaskan king crab legs are sold frozen at fish markets and full-service gourmet stores. They are easy on the cook because they are already cooked and often are sold split down the middle, which makes the meat easy to reach. Simply steam to heat the claws and legs, and serve.

For fast dipping sauces, flavor low-fat mayonnaise with a dollop or two of pesto, garlic or mustard. Melted butter seasoned generously with a seafood seasoning mix is a great accompaniment as well.

Layered Chutney Cheese Spread

This spread is delicious served on crackers or with sturdy slices of bread.
Yield: 8-10 servings

1 (8-ounce) package cream cheese, softened
3 cups shredded sharp Cheddar cheese
1/2 teaspoon curry powder
Few drops hot pepper sauce
1 (10-ounce) jar mango chutney, chopped
6 bacon strips, cooked until crisp, drained and
   crumbled
6 green onions (including green tops), chopped

1. Using a fork, stir together cream cheese, 1 1/2 cups of Cheddar cheese, curry powder and pepper sauce until combined. Spread mixture over an 8-to 10-inch serving dish, smoothing surface evenly.

2. Spread chutney over surface. Sprinkle surface with the remaining 1 1/2 cups of Cheddar, bacon and scallions. Serve with crackers and celery sticks.

3. Cover and refrigerate any leftovers.

Chevre Plate

This appetizer is a quick and easy adaptation of the
Chevre Plate served at Chapters Cafe in Orlando's College Park.
Yield: 4 appetizer servings

1 wedge or round of goat cheese
3 tablespoons bottled sun-dried tomato pesto
3 tablespoons bottled basil pesto
2 to 3 tablespoons hummus
10 to 12 (1-inch) strips roasted red peppers (see
   note)
Toasted baguette rounds

1. Place wedge of cheese in center of serving plate.

2. Dollop the pestos, hummus and roasted red pepper strips around the cheese.

3. Serve with toasted baguette rounds. Encourage guests to mash the goat cheese into the side mixtures before spreading on bread slices.

Recipe note: Bottled roasted red peppers are available in most supermarkets. Drain and puree 1 or 2 of the peppers and thinly slice to make the strips.

Potlucks, Tailgates & Picnics

Food safety tips

When you're preparing warm food that will later be placed in a cooler -fried chicken, for example - cook food hours ahead so it can cool before being packed in an ice chest. An ice chest cannot cool hot foods, and they may not get sufficiently cold to prevent spoilage.

Cold foods should be kept at 40 degrees, so pack the cooler with lots of ice. Put the cooler in the car's air-conditioned interior, not the trunk. At the beach, place the cooler under an umbrella or in the shade.

Eat carry-out foods, such as fried chicken and barbecued beef or pork, within two hours. If you have leftovers, whether it's fried chicken, pasta salad or bologna sandwiches, put them in a cooler immediately. Toss out anything that has been left out of the cooler for more than an hour. Keep cold foods in the cooler - take them out only for serving.

Potluck tips

Encourage guests to bring copies of their recipes to share with the others.

Spice up a potluck with a theme. For example, "Cheese in Every Course": nachos with cheese for appetizer, lasagna with ricotta cheese for a main dish and cheesecake for dessert.

Traveling tips

To keep sandwiches from becoming soggy en route to the park, lake or beach:

Pack moist ingredients and toppings, such as tomato slices, lettuce leaves, sliced onions, pickles and cucumbers and sprouts in sealable sandwich bags. Add the moist vegetables to the sandwiches before serving.

Spread condiments on bread or rolls just before serving.

Veggie Pockets

This is an easy, healthful picnic option. Simply stuff whole-wheat pita pockets with sprouts, shredded carrots, strips of red bell pepper and shredded romaine lettuce. Pack a bottle of ranch-style fat free dressing in the cooler with the sandwiches and let hungry beachgoers dress their own sandwiches. Shredded, low-fat cheeses can be added for heartier fare. (Tip: Gather the ingredients from the supermarket salad bar to eliminate preparation work and kitchen clean up.)

Sunrise Sampler

Don't forget breakfast on the beach for early risers. Fill a picnic basket with store-bought or homemade muffins and fresh fruit. In the cooler, stash individual serving cartons of grapefruit, orange or cranberry juice. A thermal container will keep coffee or hot tea warm. (Tip: Serve the fruit whole. Cutting it up for a salad means you would need to make additional room in the cooler and serving would require bowls and forks.)

Skewered Lunch

This translates into lunch on a stick. No plate required - just a napkin. Thread boiled shrimp on 6-inch wood skewers alternating the seafood with chunks of fresh pineapple, papaya and sprigs of fresh mint. Add cooked cheese tortellini to the mix if desired. (Tip: Boil the shrimp with a flavorful seasoning mix such as Old Bay.)

Artichoke Salad

The beauty of this easy salad is that it marinates en route.
Yield: 10-12 servings

2 (12-ounce) jars of marinated artichoke hearts
   (including liquid)
4 plum tomatoes, sliced (see note)
1 (14.4-ounce) can of hearts of palm, drained
   and sliced into rounds
Minced garlic to taste
1/2 cup chopped fresh basil

1. Coarsely chop the artichoke hearts.

2. Combine all ingredients in a bowl. Let marinate in an ice-filled cooler on the way to the beach, football game or picnic.

Recipe note: Substitute 1 large, beefsteak tomato for the plum tomatoes, if desired.

Warm Black Bean Dip for a Crowd

Serve this crowd-pleaser with plain tortilla or bagel chips
Yield: 5 cups (about 10 servings)

3 (15-ounce) cans black beans, drained and
 rinsed, divided
1/3 cup water
2 large garlic cloves
1 jalapeno pepper, seeded, chopped fine
1 teaspoon ground coriander seed
1 teaspoon salt
1/4 cup cilantro, loosely packed
1 (7 1/2 -ounce) jar roasted red peppers, drained
 and diced fine (about 2/3 cup)
6 green onions, trimmed and sliced thin, white
 and green parts separated
1 tablespoon red pepper sauce
2 tablespoons lime or lemon juice

Toppings:
Sour cream: 1 pint low-fat or nonfat sour cream,
 1/2 teaspoon chili powder or paprika, chopped
 green onions
Cheese: 8 ounces grated Monterey Jack cheese,
 chopped green onions

1. Measure 2 cups of drained black beans into a small saucepan. Add water, garlic, jalapeno, coriander and salt. Heat to boiling. Reduce heat and simmer 5 minutes.

2. Transfer bean mixture to a blender and blend until smooth. Pour the bean puree into a 2-quart casserole dish. Coarsely chop cilantro and add with the remaining whole beans, roasted peppers, white parts of the green onions, red pepper sauce and lemon juice. Stir to blend. (The dip can be prepared ahead and refrigerated up to this point.)

3. Heat oven to 250 F. While the oven is heating, prepare either the sour cream or cheese topping. If using the cheese topping, sprinkle mixture over dip, cover casserole with glass lid and place in oven for 25 minutes. If using the sour cream topping, top with mixture just before serving.

For the sour cream topping: Stir the sour cream, chili powder and scallion greens in a bowl until blended.

For the Monterey Jack cheese topping: Toss the grated cheese and chopped green onions in a small bowl.

Recipe notes: If dip is prepared in advance, heat the oven to 250 F. Remove the dip from the refrigerator and prepare one of the toppings. For the cheese topping, sprinkle the mixture over the chilled dip, cover the bowl with glass lid and bake until warmed through, about 50-60 minutes or microwave on high (100 percent power) for 5-10 minutes or until heated through.
If using the sour cream topping, heat as directed and add sour cream mixture just before serving.

Cheddar, Feta and Walnut Cheese Ball

*Cheddar, Feta and Walnut Cheese Ball is a somewhat spicy ball that combines
a creamy texture and bold flavors. This recipe was developed by the California Walnut Commission.
Yield: 2 cheese balls or logs, 12 servings*

2 cups grated Cheddar cheese
1 cup cream cheese
3/4 cup crumbled feta cheese
2 cloves garlic, minced
1/4 teaspoon salt
1/4 teaspoon hot pepper sauce
1 cup chopped walnuts, toasted (optional)
2 tablespoons capers, drained
2 tablespoons chopped, roasted and peeled red
    peppers, or 2 tablespoons chopped pimento
Pinch of cayenne pepper

*Recipe note: This cheese ball is especially good on whole-grain or rye
crackers or on thinly sliced rice bread.*

1. Combine the Cheddar cheese, cream cheese, feta cheese, garlic, salt and pepper sauce; mix until blended and smooth. Add 1/2 cup of the walnuts, capers, red peppers or pimento. Continue to mix until the ingredients are evenly blended. The mixture will be easier to shape if it is refrigerated at this point for two to three hours before forming.

2. Add a pinch of cayenne pepper to the remaining 1/2 cup walnuts. Toss to coat. Spread the nuts on a sheet of waxed paper.

3. With damp hands, divide the mixture in half. Pat and press each half into a ball about 3 inches across or into a log about 5 inches long and 2 inches wide; don't worry about keeping the shape perfect.

4. If desired, roll each ball or log in the nuts, patting the coating in firmly. Wrap in plastic wrap and chill until serving.

Tips for preparing a cheese ball

The cheeses will combine more easily if they are at room temperature, so take them out of the refrigerator a little ahead of preparation time.

The two best methods to combine cheeses are with a food processor or with your own hands. Mixing with a big wooden spoon works, but it takes a strong arm and vigorous beating. You can form the mixture into all sorts of festive shapes including cheese balls or cheese logs. You can also make individual marble-size balls. And, of course, you also can simply pack the mixture into a small bowl or crock.

Cheese balls can be made ahead and frozen. Just wrap them airtight in plastic wrap. You will need to thaw them for a couple of hours at room temperature or overnight in the refrigerator before serving.

Toss leftover pieces of the cheese ball with hot pasta or rice for a quick sauce.

Citus Slaw

This low-fat salad makes a colorful addition to your party table.
Yield: 6 (1-cup) servings

1/4 cup nonfat herbed vinaigrette
1/4 cup frozen orange juice concentrate, thawed
4 cups shredded napa cabbage
2 oranges, peeled and segmented
1 red apple, halved, cored and diced
1 cup quartered, pitted prunes
1/2 cup sliced celery
1/4 cup sliced green onions
Pepper to taste

1. In a large bowl, whisk vinaigrette and orange concentrate.

2. Add remaining ingredients except pepper. Toss thoroughly.

3. Season with pepper.

Picnic must-haves

Can/bottle opener
Cutting board
Sharp knife for fruit
Bread knife
Moistened towelettes
Garbage bags of assorted sizes for cleanup
Disposable napkins, flatware and serving pieces
First-aid kit
Insect repellent

Tarragon Shrimp and Orange Salad

This recipe was developed by the American Spice Trade Association.
Pack the salad and dressing ingredients separately in the cooler and dress the salad just before serving.
Yield: 4 servings

12 ounces cooked, shelled and deveined
   shrimp, chilled
2 cups cooked brown rice, chilled
2 cups romaine leaves torn in bite-size pieces
1 1/2 cups orange sections
1 cup halved cherry tomatoes
1/2 cup sliced red onion
1/3 cup orange tarragon dressing (see note)

1. In a large serving bowl place shrimp, rice, romaine, orange sections, cherry tomatoes and red onion.

2. Just before serving toss with orange tarragon dressing.

Recipe note: To make dressing, combine 3 tablespoons frozen orange juice concentrate, 2 tablespoons cider vinegar, 1 tablespoon olive oil, 1 teaspoon garlic powder, 1/2 teaspoon salt, 3/4 teaspoon tarragon leaves, crushed and 1/4 teaspoon ground black pepper.

Caribbean Shrimp and Mushroom Packets

The organized cook can grill this flavorful meal
while entertaining guests on the patio.
Yield: 4 servings

1 pound fresh white mushrooms, sliced
1/2 cup couscous (uncooked)
1 cup thinly sliced onion
1 cup sweet red bell pepper, chopped
1 pound extra-large shrimp, peeled and deveined
1/4 cup dry white wine
4 tablespoons butter
2 teaspoons jerk seasoning (see note)
1 teaspoon finely minced garlic
1 teaspoon salt
2 ears of corn, husked and halved

1. Heat outdoor grill to 425 F.

2. On a work surface place 4 sheets (each about 20 inches long) of heavy duty foil. In the center of each piece of foil arrange a generous 1/2 cup mushrooms, overlapping slightly; sprinkle with 2 tablespoons couscous. Top each with onion, red bell pepper, shrimp and wine, dividing evenly. Dot each with 1 tablespoon butter; sprinkle with 1/2 teaspoon jerk seasoning blend and 1/4 teaspoon each garlic and salt. Arrange remaining mushrooms over shrimp, overlapping slightly; place 1/2 an ear of corn on the side.

3. Bring long sides of foil together over mixture, allowing space for heat circulation and expansion; fold to seal. Fold up short ends; crimp to seal. Place on grill, about 5 inches from heat.

4. Cook until shrimp are done, about 15 minutes, turning once. Place in individual serving bowls; carefully unfold foil.

Recipe note: Jerk seasoning is available in supermarkets. If unavailable, substitute 1 teaspoon sugar and 1/4 teaspoon each thyme, allspice and ground red pepper.

Muffuletta

Frequent visitors to New Orleans know the trip isn't complete without a stop at Central Grocery for a muffuletta. Once you've tasted one, it's hard to go back to an ordinary sandwich.

Yield: 4-6 servings

1 (9 3/4 -ounce) jar green olive salad, drained and chopped
1/4 cup pitted black olives, chopped
1 large celery stalk, finely chopped
1 1/2 teaspoons Tabasco, divided
1 (8-inch) round loaf of crusty French or sourdough bread
3 tablespoons olive oil
1/4 pound sliced salami
1/4 pound sliced baked ham
1/4 pound sliced Provolone cheese

1. In a medium bowl, combine green olive salad, chopped, pitted black olives, celery and 1 teaspoon of Tabasco.

2. Cut bread in half crosswise. Remove some of the soft inside from each half.

3. In a small bowl, combine olive oil and remaining Tabasco. Brush mixture on inside of bread halves. Fill bottom with olive mixture. Layer salami, ham and provolone slices on top of olive mixture. Top with other bread half. Cut loaf into quarters.

Tex-Italian Pasta Fiesta

This a tantalizing blend of flavors. A salad and bread complete the meal.
Yield: 8 servings

8 ounces mostaccioli pasta
1 (10-ounce) package frozen chopped spinach, thawed
1 (8-ounce) package reduced-fat cream cheese, softened
1/2 cup milk
1 teaspoon dried oregano
1 pound lean ground beef
2 cloves garlic, minced
2 cups Pace Picante Sauce
1 (8-ounce) can tomato sauce
1 (6-ounce) can tomato paste
2 teaspoons chili powder
1 1/2 teaspoons ground cumin
1 cup shredded mozzarella or Cheddar cheese
Ripe olive slices (optional)
Green onion slices (optional)

1. Heat oven to 350 F. Cook pasta according to package directions; drain and rinse with cold water. Squeeze spinach dry.

2. Combine spinach, cream cheese, milk and oregano; mix well.

3. Brown ground beef with garlic; drain. To the browned beef, add cooked pasta, picante sauce, tomato paste, tomato sauce and seasonings; mix well.

4. Spoon half the pasta mixture into a lightly greased 13-by-9-inch baking dish. Top evenly with spinach mixture. Top with remaining pasta mixture. Cover loosely with foil; bake 30 minutes. Uncover and sprinkle with shredded cheese; continue baking 2 minutes. Let stand 10 minutes. Top as desired and served with additional picante sauce.

Nature's Table Vegetarian Chili

This chili freezes well. Make it ahead of time and reheat at your tailgate or picnic site.
Yield: 10 servings

1 (2-pound) can Heinz tomato sauce
1 (2-pound) can kidney beans, drained
1 large green bell pepper, seeded and chopped
1 medium-size onion, peeled and chopped
2 fresh tomatoes, cut in small chunks
1 carrot, cleaned and grated
2 tablespoons chili powder
1 tablespoon Spike All-Purpose Seasoning
1 tablespoon dried sweet basil
Shredded white Cheddar cheese for garnish
  (optional)

1. In a large kettle or stockpot, mix all ingredients except shredded cheese.

2. Bring ingredients to a simmer and cook for 1 1/2 hours, stirring occasionally.

3. Serve with grated cheese.

Cheesy Cornbread

Serve this four-ingredient bread with Nature's Table Vegetarian Chili.
Yield: 12 servings

1/2 cup finely chopped sweet onion
2 tablespoons butter or margarine
2 (10-ounce) packages corn bread mix
1 cup shredded sharp Cheddar cheese

1. In a skillet, cook onion in butter or margarine until tender but not brown.

2. Heat oven to 375 F. Prepare corn bread mix according to package directions. Stir in cooked onion and shredded cheese.

3. Pour batter into greased a 3-quart oblong baking dish (13-by-9-by-2 inches). Bake until done, about 30 minutes.

Southwest Pepperjack Sandwich

Pepper-flavored cheese adds a kick to this tailgate sandwich.
Regular Monterey Jack can be substituted for more timid fare.
Yield: 8 servings

1 3/4 cups (7 ounces) shredded hot-pepper
   Monterey Jack cheese
2 1/2 cups buttermilk baking mix
1/2 cup cornmeal
1/2 cup frozen corn kernels, thawed
1 cup milk
4 ounces shredded Cheddar cheese
4 ounces sliced baked ham
Lettuce leaves

1. Heat oven to 450 F. Butter and lightly flour a small baking sheet; set aside. In a large bowl, stir together 1 1/2 cups of the Monterey Jack cheese along with the baking mix, cornmeal and corn. Add milk; stir just until a dough is formed.

2. Sprinkle work surface with additional baking mix or flour; place dough on work surface; lightly knead, 8 to 10 times. Shape into ball; place on prepared baking sheet. Roll or pat dough into an 8-inch circle about 3/4-inch thick. Use a sharp knife, cut into 8 wedges.

3. Sprinkle wedges with the remaining 1/4 cup Monterey Jack cheese. Bake until golden brown, 15 to 17 minutes. Remove to wire rack. Cool completely.

4. To prepare sandwiches, cut each wedge in half horizontally. Cut Cheddar cheese and ham to fit over 1 of the wedges. Top with lettuce, then the other wedge half. Repeat with other wedges.

Touchdown Beef and Honey Mustard Sandwich

Yield: 6 servings

1/2 cup light sour cream
1 tablespoon Dijon-style mustard
1 tablespoon honey
1 pound long-loaf French or Italian bread, or
   two 1/2 -pound long loaves, split lengthwise
6 lettuce leaves
1 cup deli coleslaw, creamy-style
1 pound thinly sliced deli roast beef
1 large tomato, thinly sliced

1. Combine sour cream, mustard and honey; mix well. Spread on cut slices of bread. Arrange lettuce leaves on top of sour cream mixture. Spread coleslaw evenly over lettuce leaves.

2. Top with roast beef and tomato. Close with top half of loaf. Wrap in aluminum foil. Refrigerate up to 4 hours. Carry to site in insulated cooler.

3. To serve, cut into slices.

Triple Treat Bean Salad

This bean salad is great for toting to a football game or serving at a summer pool party.
Yield: 12 servings

1 (15-ounce) can garbanzo beans, drained, rinsed
1 (15-ounce) can pinto beans, drained, rinsed
1 (15-ounce) can black beans, drained, rinsed
3/4 cup chopped sweet red pepper
1/4 cup chopped cilantro
1/4 cup sliced green onions
1 clove garlic, minced
1 (8-ounce) package low-fat shredded Cheddar
   cheese
Hot pepper sauce to taste

1. Combine ingredients; mix lightly. Chill several hours to blend flavors.

2. Keep the mixture chilled in a cooler until ready to serve.

Spiral Sandwiches

Armenian cracker bread (also called lavosh) is a flatbread that keeps well.
Look for lavosh in the bread or cracker section of your supermarket or in a specialty food shop
that carries Middle Eastern products. If you can't find it, substitute large flour tortillas.
Yield: 6 servings

15-inch sesame seed Armenian cracker bread
1/2 of an 8-ounce package light cream cheese
  (Neufchatel), softened
1 tablespoon snipped fresh basil or 1 teaspoon dried
  basil, crushed
1 tablespoon snipped fresh oregano or 1 teaspoon
  dried oregano, crushed
1/4 teaspoon salt
1/4 teaspoon garlic powder
1/8 teaspoon pepper
4 ounces very thinly sliced, fully cooked smoked
  turkey or ham
1 large tomato, very thinly sliced
2 ounces very thinly sliced Monterey Jack or Swiss
  cheese
1/2 cup alfalfa sprouts
1 large romaine lettuce leaf, rib removed

1. Dampen cracker bread on both sides by holding the bread briefly under gently running cold water. Place the moistened bread between two damp clean cloth towels, making sure the sesame seed side is facing down. Let the bread stand at room temperature about 1 hour or until it has softened for rolling.

2. In a mixing bowl combine the cream cheese, basil, oregano, salt, garlic powder and pepper. Use a fork to stir until mixed.

3. Uncover the softened bread, leaving it on the bottom towel. Using a spatula or table knife, gently spread the cream cheese filling onto the bread. Arrange the turkey or ham slices in a layer atop the cream cheese mixture. Top the meat slices with a layer of tomatoes. Top the tomatoes with a layer of Monterey Jack or Swiss cheese. Sprinkle with alfalfa sprouts.

4. Place the lettuce leaf along one of the short sides of the bread, on top of the alfalfa sprouts. Starting on the side with the lettuce and using the towel to lift, roll up the bread, jellyroll style, so that the sesame seeds are on the outside of the roll. Cover and chill the roll, seam side down, for 2 to 24 hours. To serve, trim uneven edges. Cut the chilled roll into 1-inch-thick slices.

Glazed Pecans

Nut mixes travel well and are great snacks to put out while putting together the tailgate spread.
Yield: 2 cups

1 cup sugar
1/4 cup orange juice
2 cups pecan halves
Solid shortening

1. Grease a large sheet of aluminum foil with solid shortening.

2. In a large bowl, mix together sugar and orange juice. Add nuts, stirring to coat completely. Pour into a microwave-safe shallow pan.

3. Cook on 60 percent (medium) power for 6 minutes. Remove pan and stir. Microwave a 60 percent power for 6 more minutes. Do not stir.

4. Pour pecans out onto the greased foil. Carefully spread apart into a single layer. Cool completely. Break apart and store in a covered container.

Cajun Pork Roast

Yield: 6 to 8 servings.

2 pound boneless single-loin pork roast or
  1 rolled and tied double-loin roast
3 tablespoons paprika
1/2 teaspoon cayenne pepper
1 tablespoon garlic powder
2 teaspoons oregano
2 teaspoons thyme
1/2 tablespoon salt
1/2 teaspoon white pepper
1/2 teaspoon cumin
1/2 teaspoon nutmeg

1. Heat oven to 350 F.

2. Combine all seasonings and rub well over all surfaces of roast. Place meat in a shallow pan and roast in oven for about an hour, until internal temperature is 155-160 F. If roasting a double loin, cooking time will be longer.

3. Remove roast from oven, let rest 5 to 10 minutes before slicing. Refrigerate and serve cold at a tailgate or picnic party.

Turkey Sandwich With Artichoke Relish

This recipe is similar to the Muffuletta on page 45. The sandwich has a slightly milder flavor because it uses chopped artichoke

1 (6-ounce) jar marinated artichoke hearts, chopped
1/2 cup pimento-stuffed green olives, chopped
1/2 cup pitted black olives, chopped
1/3 cup roasted red peppers, cut in large pieces
3 cloves garlic, pressed
1/4 cup chopped parsley
1 cup extra-virgin olive oil
3 tablespoons red-wine vinegar
1/2 teaspoon coarsely ground black pepper
6 sourdough sandwich rolls
3/4 pound smoked turkey breast, sliced
3/4 pound Provolone cheese, sliced

1. In a medium bowl, combine artichoke hearts, olives, red peppers, garlic, chopped parsley, olive oil, vinegar and pepper. Cover tightly and refrigerate artichoke-olive relish overnight.

2. At the tailgate site, slice sandwich rolls horizontally. Remove some of the center of the bread halves.

3. Drizzle olive oil from refrigerated artichoke relish heavily on the sides of all the bread slices. On the six bottom halves of bread layer turkey and cheese and artichoke relish. Top with other halves of bread. Cut sandwiches in half and serve.

Spinach-Artichoke Lasagna

No-boil lasagna noodles make quick work of this lasagna.
Yield: 12 servings

2 (10-ounce) packages frozen chopped spinach, thawed
2 (8 1/2-ounce can artichoke hearts, drained and coarsely chopped
1 (15-ounce) container low-fat ricotta
1 (8-ounce) package grated, low-fat mozzarella cheese
1 cup grated Parmesan cheese, divided
2 egg whites
1/4 teaspoon ground black pepper
1/8 teaspoon ground nutmeg
6 1/2 cups marinara sauce, divided
1 (8-ounce) package no-boil lasagna noodles

1. Squeeze as much liquid from the spinach and artichokes as possible. Place them in a large bowl. Add the ricotta, mozzarella, 1/2 cup of the Parmesan, egg whites, black pepper and nutmeg. Stir until blended.

2. Pour 1 cup of the marinara sauce in an even layer over the bottom of a 9-by-13-inch baking pan. Top with 3 pieces of lasagna (side-by-side, not overlapping). Spread 1 cup of the marinara sauce over the noodles and top with a third of the ricotta mixture. Spread 1/2 cup of the tomato sauce over that mixture.

3. Repeat making two more layers of noodles-sauce-filling-sauce. Top with a layer of noodles. Spread remaining marinara sauce over the noodles. The lasagna can be prepared up to two days in advance at this point. Cover and pan refrigerate until ready to bake.

4. Heat oven to 350 F. Cover lasagna with foil. Bake until the edges are bubbling vigorously and the center is piping hot, about 45 minutes to 1 hour. Remove the foil. Sprinkle remaining Parmesan cheese over the top. Bake 15 minutes longer. Let rest 10 minutes before serving.

Honey-Mustard Glazed Chicken Wings
With Scallion-Sesame Confetti

Yield: About 50 pieces

About 25 whole chicken wings
1/2 cup honey
1/2 cup orange juice
6 tablespoons prepared mustard
2 tablespoons soy sauce
1/2 teaspoon hot red pepper sauce
3 green onions, thinly sliced
2 tablespoons sesame seeds

1. Heat oven to 375 F. Cut off and discard wing tips. Cut remaining wings into 2 pieces at joints. Spray 13-by-9-inch baking dish with nonstick spray. Arrange wings in 2 layers.

2. Bake for 30 minutes, stirring after 20 minutes. Remove as much oil as possible.

3. Heat honey, orange juice, mustard, soy and red pepper sauce to boiling for 5 minutes. Pour over wings.

4. Return baking dish to oven. Bake, stirring, until wings are lightly browned, about 40-50 minutes.

5. Sprinkle green onions and sesame seeds over wings. Stir to coat.

You don't have to spend big bucks on picnic hampers and basketry for collegiate tailgate parties. Simply spray paint inexpensive baskets with your school colors.

If the picnic basket has a flat lid, apply a decal of your team's logo for a custom look.

Jambalaya

Yield: 12 servings

1/4 cup oil
1 chicken, cut up and deboned
Salt to taste
Pepper to taste
1 1/2 pounds andouille sausage
4 cups chopped sweet onions
2 cups chopped celery
2 cups chopped green bell peppers
2 tablespoons chopped garlic
7 cups chicken broth, divided
Cayenne pepper to taste
4 cups long-grain rice
2 cups chopped green onions
2 cups chopped tomatoes

1. Heat oil in a large pot over medium-high heat. Season chicken to taste with salt and pepper. Brown chicken in hot oil. Add sausage and saute with chicken. With a slotted spoon, remove chicken and sausage from pot.

2. Reheat remaining oil and saute onions, celery, green peppers and garlic to desired tenderness. Return chicken and sausage to pot. Add 5 cups of the stock, 2 teaspoons salt, cayenne pepper and bring to a boil.

3. Add rice and return mixture to a boil. Cover and simmer for 10 minutes. Remove cover and quickly and thoroughly stir rice. Add green onions and tomatoes. Cover and cook until rice is tender, about 25 minutes. Add additional broth as needed.

Special Occasions & Celebrations

Special occasions

1. New Year's
2. Brunch
3. Purim
4. Easter
5. Showers, Teas and Christening Receptions
6. Fourth of July
7. Halloween
8. Thanksgiving
9. Holiday Dinner Party
10. Kwanzaa

Menu suggestions for other celebrations

1. Derby Day Party
2. Mardi Gras
3. Rosh Hashana
4. Graduation Dinner
5. Basketball Playoff Party
6. Bowl Game Tailgate
7. Holiday Cookie Exchange
8. Apres Theater/Concert Gathering

New Year's Celebration

Menu
Polenta Bites, Hoppin' John,
Citrus Spinach Salad, sliced Cuban bread, store-bought pie or cake,
Sparkling Water or Wine with Carambola Cubes

Polenta Bites

Yield: 36 appetizers

Vegetable cooking spray
2 (14 1/2-ounce) cans reduced-sodium chicken
   broth
1 cup yellow cornmeal
1/3 cup dried tomato bits or dried tomato halves
   snipped into small pieces
1/2 cup grated Parmesan cheese
3 tablespoons olive oil

1. Coat a 9-by-13-inch baking pan with vegetable cooking spray.

2. Line the pan with plastic wrap, allowing long sides to extend over the edges.

3. In a saucepan, bring broth to a boil. Whisk in cornmeal and tomato bits. Reduce heat and simmer, whisking constantly for about 5 minutes until the mixture is very thick. Remove pan from heat and stir in cheese until thoroughly blended.

4. Spread polenta in plastic-lined pan. Cover loosely with wax paper. Refrigerate for at least 1 hour, or preferably overnight.

5. Lifting edges of plastic wrap, remove polenta from the pan to a cutting board. Cut into squares, diamonds or rectangles, or cut into star shapes with cookie cutters.

6. Heat broiler. Place polenta pieces on a baking sheet. Brush polenta lightly with olive oil. Place about 4 inches below heat source. Broil 1 minute or just until lightly browned, watching closely. Serve warm.

Hoppin' John

Yield: 8 servings

1 pound meaty ham hocks
1 cup chopped sweet onion
2 teaspoons salt
1/4 teaspoon crushed red pepper
1 jalapeno, seeded and chopped (optional)
3 1/2 cups water
2 cups dry black-eyed peas
1 1/2 cups uncooked rice
Salt and ground black pepper
Tabasco sauce to taste

1. Combine ham hocks, onion, salt, red pepper, jalapeno and water in large saucepan. Bring to a boil, cover and simmer 1 1/4 hours, or until ham is tender.

2. Wash black-eyed peas. Combine black-eyed peas and 6 cups water; bring to boil and boil 2 minutes. Remove from heat, cover and let stand 1 hour. Remove ham hocks from saucepan. Add water to liquid left in saucepan to measure 3 1/2 cups, if necessary.

3. Cut meat into small pieces, discarding bone and rind. Drain peas; discard soaking liquid.

4. Combine ham, black-eyed peas and rice in large saucepan; bring mixture to a boil. Reduce heat, cover and simmer 20-25 minutes, or until peas and rice are tender and liquid is absorbed. Season to taste with salt, black pepper and Tabasco.

Spinach Citrus Salad

Yield: 12 servings

2 pounds fresh spinach leaves
1 (8-ounce) can mandarin oranges, drained
1 (8-ounce) can sliced water chestnuts, drained
1 small red onion, peeled, sliced and separated
   into rings
4 tablespoons vegetable oil
3 tablespoons sugar
3 tablespoons ketchup
3 tablespoons cider vinegar
2 tablespoons orange juice
2 teaspoons Worcestershire sauce
Salt and pepper to taste

1. Clean spinach leaves; tear into bite-sized pieces. In a large bowl, combine spinach, oranges, water chestnuts and onion rings. Cover and chill, if made ahead.

2. Stir together the remaining ingredients well. When ready to serve, toss salad with dressing.

Carambola Cubes

Yield: 12 garnishes for beverages

2 carambolas (star fruit)

1. Slice each carambola into 6 slices.

2. Freeze slices on a baking sheet.

3. Plop a slice into a glass of sparkling wine or water and serve.

Brunch

Menu
Jill's Egg Strata, Festive Hash Browns,
Glazed Canadian Bacon, Fruit Kebabs,
Quick Phyllo Pudding Tarts, assorted fruit juices, coffee

Jill's Egg Strata

Yield: 6 -8 servings

8 slices of Challah bread, trimmed and cubed
1/2 pound grated Cheddar cheese
4 eggs
1 teaspoon prepared mustard
1/2 teaspoon salt
1/2 teaspoon pepper
2 cups milk
1/2 stick margarine, melted

1. Layer bread cubes and grated Cheddar cheese in a buttered 2-quart casserole dish.

2. In a large bowl, lightly beat eggs and stir in remaining ingredients. Pour mixture over bread and refrigerate overnight.

3. Heat oven to 350 F. Bake for 1 hour and serve.

Festive Hash Browns

Yield: 6 servings

1 (1-pound, 4-ounce) package refrigerated home-style shredded hash brown potatoes
For a Christmas brunch: 1 green bell pepper, 1 red bell pepper, chopped
For a Spring brunch: 1 green bell pepper, 1 yellow bell pepper chopped
1/2 cup chopped sweet onion
1/4 to 1/2 cup shredded Parmesan cheese
1/2 teaspoon salt
1/4 teaspoon pepper
1 tablespoon margarine, melted
1 tablespoon vegetable oil
Additional Parmesan cheese (optional)

1. Heat oven to 325 F.

2. Toss potatoes, bell peppers, onion, 1/4 to 1/2 cup Parmesan cheese, salt and pepper.

3. Pour margarine and oil into a 13-by-9-by-2-inch baking pan. Spread potato mixture in pan.

4. Bake, uncovered, about 25 minutes, stirring once, until golden brown. Sprinkle with additional Parmesan cheese to taste before serving.

Glazed Canadian Bacon

Yield: 6 servings

1 (8-ounce) package sliced Canadian bacon
1/4 cup packed brown sugar
1 tablespoon Dijon mustard

1. Heat oven to 325 F. Place bacon slices on a large piece of heavy-duty aluminum foil.

2. Mix brown sugar and mustard. Spoon mixture over bacon. Wrap bacon in foil and place on a baking sheet.

3. Bake for 30 minutes or until hot.

Fruit Kebabs

Yield 6 (2-kebab) servings

12 (6-inch) wooden skewers
12 large, washed, stemmed and halved
  strawberries
24 pineapple chunks
12 frozen peach slices, cut in half
12 mint leaves

1. On each skewer, thread a strawberry half, pineapple chunk, peach halve and mint leaf. Repeat with fruit only.

Recipe note: For an adult twist, marinate the kebabs in spiced rum overnight.

Quick Phyllo Pudding Tarts

Yield: 12 tarts, 6 servings

12-pack frozen mini phyllo shells, thawed
1 cup favorite vanilla pudding
12 washed blueberries or raspberries

1. Spoon about a tablespoon of pudding into each phyllo shell.

2. Top with a blueberry or raspberry and serve.

Purim

Menu
Eggplant Spread, Chicken with Asparagus
on Pasta, Poppy Seed Hamantaschen

Eggplant Spread

Yield: 12-14 appetizer servings

2 medium eggplants
1/8 bunch fresh dill
Juice of 1/4 lemon
1 1/2 teaspoons olive oil
1 cup mayonnaise
1/8 tablespoon salt
1/8 tablespoon white pepper
1 tablespoon fresh garlic that has been minced
   or crushed in a garlic press
1 loaf French bread, sliced thinly and toasted
   under the broiler

1. Heat oven to 375 F.

2. Pierce eggplants with fork. Put eggplants on a baking sheet and place in heated oven. Bake for 1 hour until tender. When the eggplants are cool enough to handle cut them in half and remove the peel. Cube remaining eggplant meat.

3. Place eggplant cubes and remainder of ingredients in a blender or food processor container and process until smooth.

4. Serve with toasted bread rounds.

Poppy Seed Hamantaschen

Yield: About 3 dozen cookies

5 to 6 cups flour, divided
1/2 teaspoon salt
1 teaspoon baking powder
1/2 cup shortening
5 eggs, divided
1 cup honey
Poppy seed filling:
2 cups poppy seeds
1 cup milk
3/4 cup honey
1 teaspoon lemon peel
1/2 cup raisins

1. To make filling, grind 2 cups poppy seeds. Combine ground seeds with 1 cup milk and 3/4 cup honey. Cook over low heat until thickened. Add 1 teaspoon lemon peel and 1/2 cup raisins. Cool.

2. Heat oven to 350F. Combine 5 cups flour, salt and baking powder; mix well. Make a well in the center and add shortening, 4 eggs and honey. Work together until dough is formed, adding flour as needed. Roll out thinly and cut into 4-inch circles.

3. Place 1 tablespoon poppy seed filling on each; fold up three sides and press together into triangles leaving tops somewhat open. Beat remaining egg and brush over dough. Bake for 20 minutes or until browned.

Chicken With Asparagus

Yield: 4 servings

1/4 cup instant minced onion
1 tablespoon vegetable oil
1 pound fresh asparagus, cut in 1-inch pieces
  (about 3 cups)
1 1/4 cups diced sweet red bell pepper
12 ounces boned and skinned chicken breasts,
  cut in 1-inch pieces
1 1/4 cups orange juice, divided
1 teaspoon cornstarch
1 teaspoon tarragon leaves, crushed
1/4 teaspoon salt
1/8 teaspoon ground black pepper

1. In a small cup combine onion and 1/4 cup water; set aside for 10 minutes to soften.

2. In a large nonstick skillet over medium high heat, heat oil until hot; add asparagus and red pepper; cook, stirring constantly, until nearly crisp-tender, about 3 minutes. Add chicken and reserved onion mixture; cook, stirring constantly, until chicken is cooked through.

3. In a small bowl combine until smooth 1/4 cup orange juice and cornstarch; stir into skillet along with remaining 1 cup orange juice, tarragon, salt and black pepper; cook, stirring constantly, 1 minute longer.

Recipe note: Serve over hot, cooked fettucine and garnish with orange slices.

Easter

Menu
Artichokes with Garbanzo Dip,
Store-bought honey-baked ham, Roasted Vidalia Onions,
steamed green beans, Greek Trinity Bread and Strawberries
and Dipping Sauces (recipes page 106)

Artichokes With Garbanzo Dip

Yield: 8 servings

8 medium artichokes
2 (15 1/2-ounce) cans reduced-sodium garbanzo
   beans
1/2 cup lemon juice
2 teaspoons minced garlic
1 tablespoon olive oil
1 teaspoon freshly grated lemon peel
1/4 cup finely chopped parsley
1/2 cup thinly sliced green onions
1/2 teaspoon crushed, dried oregano

1. Cut off stem at base of each artichoke; remove small bottom leaves. If desired, trim tips of leaves and cut off top 2 inches of artichokes. Stand artichokes upright in deep saucepan. Add 2 inches to 3 inches boiling water. Cover; boil gently 35 to 45 minutes (until base pierces easily with a fork). Drain.

2. Drain garbanzo beans, reserving 6 tablespoons of liquid in each can.

3. In the work bowl of a food processor, combine garbanzo beans, reserved liquid, lemon juice, garlic and olive oil. (If the work bowl isn't big enough for the ingredients, do this in two batches.) Process mixture until smooth. Transfer mixture to a large mixing bowl and stir in the lemon peel, parsley, green onion and oregano. Cover and refrigerate until ready to use. Serve as a dip with artichokes.

Roasted Vidalia Onions With Vinaigrette

Yield: 8 servings

4 large Vidalia onions, peeled, ends removed
4 tablespoons olive oil
1/4 cup freshly chopped parsley
Freshly ground black pepper and salt to taste
8 sprigs of fresh parsley for garnish
Vinaigrette:
2 tablespoons coarse-grained mustard
2 tablespoons red-wine vinegar
1/2 cup olive oil
2 tablespoons chopped parsley
Salt and freshly ground black pepper to taste

1. Heat oven to 400 F.

2. Cut onions in half. Trim round end of each onion half so that it will sit flat. Cut an "X" across each onion surface. Place the finished onions in a shallow baking dish.

3. In a small bowl, combine 4 tablespoons olive oil and 1/4 cup freshly chopped parsley. Drizzle the mixture across and into the onions. Season with salt and pepper to taste.

4. Place dish in oven and bake until onions are tender, about 45 minutes to an hour.

5. While onions are in oven, combine mustard and red-wine vinegar. Whisk in the olive oil. Stir in the remaining parsley. Season to taste with salt and pepper.

6. Remove onions from the oven and let cool for 10 minutes.

7. Drizzle vinaigrette over onions and serve with a sprig of fresh parsley.

Greek Trinity Bread

Yield: 1 loaf

3 to 3 1/2 cups all-purpose flour
1/4 cup sugar
2 packages RapidRise Yeast
1 teaspoon anise seed
1 teaspoon salt
1/2 cup water
1/3 cup butter or margarine, cut up
3 eggs, divided use
1 cup golden raisins

1. In large bowl, combine 1 cup flour, sugar, undissolved yeast, anise seed and salt. Heat water and butter until very warm (120 to 130 F); stir into dry ingredients. Stir in 2 eggs, 1 egg yolk (reserve egg white) and enough remaining flour to make soft dough. Knead on lightly floured surface until smooth and elastic, about 5 to 7 minutes. Cover; let rest 10 minutes.

2. Remove 1/2 cup dough; reserve. Knead raisins into remaining dough; divide into 3 equal pieces. Form each into smooth ball; arrange on greased baking sheet in the shape of a three-leaf clover. Divide reserved dough into 4 equal pieces; roll each to 10-inch rope. Place 2 ropes side by side; twist together, pinching ends to seal. Repeat with remaining ropes. Arrange twisted ropes on clover in the form of a cross, tucking ends under. Cover; let rise in warm, draft-free place until doubled in size, about 45 to 60 minutes.

3. Lightly beat reserved egg white; brush on dough. Bake at 375 F for 30 to 35 minutes or until done, covering with foil after 10 minutes to prevent excess browning. Remove from pan; cool on wire rack.

Showers, Teas and Christening Receptions

Menu
Watercress and Smoked Salmon Sandwiches,
Artichoke-Shrimp Casserole, green salad,
supermarket deli pasta salad, Fruit Tarts with Citrus Curd,
Minted Citrus Punch (recipe page 118)

Watercress and Smoked Salmon Sandwiches

Yield: 20 appetizer sandwiches

5 ounces smoked salmon or trout chopped
3 ounces light cream cheese, softened
2 teaspoons lemon juice
1 teaspoon Worcestershire sauce
Hot pepper sauce to taste
8 slices pumpernickel or whole-wheat bread,
   crusts trimmed
1 bunch watercress, stems removed

1. In the work bowl of a food processor, combine smoked salmon, cream cheese, lemon juice, Worcestershire sauce and hot pepper sauce to taste. Process until mixture is smooth.

2. Transfer mixture to a bowl, cover and refrigerate. Spread bread slices with salmon mixture.

3. Arrange watercress sprigs on 4 of the slices and top with remaining bread slices.

4. Cut into quarters or triangles, or use cookie cutters such as hearts and fluted circles to make assorted sandwich shapes. Arrange on serving platter.

Artichoke-Shrimp Casserole

Yield: 6-8 servings

6 1/2 tablespoons butter, divided
4 1/2 tablespoons flour
3/4 cup milk
3/4 cup heavy cream
Salt and pepper to taste
1 (14-ounce) can artichoke hearts, drained
1 pound cooked shrimp
1/4 pound fresh mushrooms, sliced
1/2 to 1 cup sherry (not cooking sherry)
1 tablespoon Worcestershire sauce
1/4 cup freshly grated Parmesan cheese
Paprika

1. Heat oven to 375F.

2. Melt 4 tablespoons of butter and stir in flour. Add milk and cream stirring with wire whisk. Cook over medium heat until thickened.

3. Slice artichoke hearts in half and arrange on the bottom of a buttered baking dish. Scatter shrimp over artichokes.

4. Cook mushrooms in remaining butter for 6 minutes. Add to casserole.

5. Add sherry and Worcestershire sauce to cream sauce and pour over contents of baking dish.

6. Sprinkle with Parmesan cheese and paprika. Bake 20-30 minutes.

Fruit Tarts With Citrus Curd

Yield: 12 tarts

Citrus Curd:
1/3 cup orange juice
1/4 cup fresh lemon juice
1 teaspoon each grated orange and lemon rind
3 egg yolks
1/2 cup granulated sugar
1 tablespoon cornstarch
3 tablespoons butter, softened
12 (3-inch) baked tart shells
1 1/2 cups fresh fruit such as halved and seeded
   grapes, kiwi slices, sliced strawberries, raspberries
   and mandarin orange sections
12 mint sprigs for garnish

1. In a small saucepan, stir together orange juice, lemon juice, grated citrus rind, egg yolks, sugar and cornstarch until smooth; add butter. Cook over medium-low heat, whisking constantly, for 3 to 5 minutes or until mixture comes to a full boil and thickens.

2. Let cool slightly, place in covered container or jar and refrigerate for up to 5 days.

3. Shortly before serving, spread citrus curd evenly in baked shells and arrange fresh fruits on top. Garnish with mint sprigs.

Fourth of July

Menu
Grilled chicken or ribs basted with Desert Flower Whiskey Sauce
or Peachy Chinese Barbecue Sauce, Macaroni and Cheese With a Twist, Potato Salad and
Artichoke Salad (recipe page 37), box mix brownies.

Macaroni and Cheese With a Twist

Yield: 10-12 servings

1 pound elbow macaroni, twists, rotini or rigatoni
2 tablespoons margarine
6 tablespoons all-purpose flour
2 cups skim milk
1 1/2 cups (6 ounces) grated Cheddar cheese
1/4 teaspoon cayenne pepper
1 teaspoon salt
1/3 cup grated Parmesan cheese

Variation 1: Melt 2 tablespoons margarine in a large skillet. Add 1 cup dry bread crumbs; saute until lightly toasted. Sprinkle bread crumbs over casserole before baking.

Variation 2: Stir 1 cup frozen vegetables, such as peas, corn, lima beans or succotash, into the cheese sauce.

Variation 3: Stir two diced tomatoes and 2 tablespoons canned, chopped jalapenos into the cheese sauce.

Variation 4: Add 1 cup cottage cheese, 1/2 cup low-fat sour cream or 1/2 cup yogurt to the cheese sauce.

Variation 5: Add 1 tablespoon chopped fresh herbs, or 1/2 teaspoon dried herbs, such as thyme, oregano, savory or basil, and 2 tablespoons chopped fresh parsley to the cheese sauce.

1. Prepare pasta according to package directions; drain and rinse under cold water. Set pasta aside. Heat oven to 375 F.

2. In a medium saucepan, melt margarine over low heat. Stir in flour with a whisk and cook, stirring for 1 minute. Gradually whisk in the milk; bring the sauce to a boil, stirring constantly. Remove from heat and add Cheddar cheese, cayenne pepper and salt. Stir until cheese has melted.

3. In a large mixing bowl, stir the cheese sauce and pasta together. Spoon into a 1 1/2 -quart ovenproof casserole dish. Sprinkle the Parmesan cheese over the top. Bake in a 375 F oven until browned on top and hot all the way through, about 30 to 35 minutes.

Desert Flower Whiskey Sauce

Yield: about 1 cup

1/4 tablespoon butter
2 green onions
3 tablespoons dark brown sugar
2 ounces Jack Daniels whiskey
1 cup ketchup
1/4 teaspoon vinegar
3/4 teaspoon hot red pepper sauce

1. Using the firm white/light green part of the onions only, chop fine. Saute onions in the melted butter until onions begin to brown.

2. Turn the burner to low and add brown sugar. Stir until sugar darkens and clumps up. Be careful not to burn!

3. Turn the burner off and add the whiskey. Stir until the sugar is completely melted.

4. Add the remaining items, mixing until the whiskey is well-incorporated. Heat on medium-low for 15 minutes. Stir as needed.

Peachy Chinese Barbecue Sauce

Yield: about 2 cups

1/2 cup chopped onion
2 cloves garlic, crushed
2 tablespoons Asian sesame oil
1 (12-ounce) jar peach or apricot preserves
1/4 cup ketchup-based chili sauce
1/3 cup red-wine vinegar
1 teaspoon hickory salt or table salt
2 teaspoons soy sauce

1. Saute the onion and garlic in oil in a small saucepan until tender. Stir in the preserves, chili sauce, vinegar, hickory salt and soy sauce.

2. Simmer for 20 minutes. Serve with chicken or pork.

Potato Salad

Yield: 8 servings

3 pounds small red new potatoes
2 tablespoons seasoned rice vinegar
Salt, freshly ground pepper
2 tablespoons plain low-fat yogurt
1 tablespoon reduced-fat mayonnaise
1 1/2 teaspoons honey mustard
1 tablespoon minced fresh chives
1 tablespoon minced fresh tarragon

1. Put potatoes in a large pot of cold water and bring to a boil. Cook potatoes just until they can easily be pierced with tip of a sharp knife, about 8-12 minutes. Drain. When the potatoes are cool enough to handle but still hot, cut in half and place in a large bowl. Toss with vinegar, salt and pepper and set aside to cool.

2. Mix yogurt, mayonnaise and mustard in a small dish. Add to potatoes along with herbs and mix lightly. Add additional salt and pepper to taste.

3. Serve or chill until serving time.

Halloween

Menu
Feijoada, Cheesy Cornbread (recipe page 48),
Caesar Salad, Brownie Banana Split Pizza

Feijoada

Yield: 12 servings

1 pound dried black beans
Water to cover bean, plus
6 cups water
1 pound boneless ham, cut into 3/4 -inch cubes
1 pound boneless pork loin, cut into 3/4 -inch cubes
3/4 pound hot Italian sausage, sliced into 1-inch pieces
3/4 pound smoked sausage, sliced into 1-inch pieces
1 pint cherry tomatoes, stemmed
1 onion, peeled and chopped
1 teaspoon red pepper flakes
6 cloves garlic, peeled and minced
1/8 teaspoon grated orange rind

1. Cover the beans with water and soak overnight. Or cover the beans with boiling water, and let stand two hours. Drain.

2. Heat oven to 350 F.

3. In a large Dutch oven, combine beans, the 6 cups water and remaining ingredients. Bring to a boil, skimming surface if necessary. Cover and transfer to oven.

4. Bake 1 1/2 hours. Remove cover and bake another 30 minutes, stirring occasionally. Serve immediately, with cornbread, if desired.

Caesar Salad

Yield: 8-10 servings

3 hard-boiled egg yolks (see note)
6 ounces olive oil
5 anchovy fillets, crushed
1 1/2 ounces red-wine vinegar
1/2 tablespoon Worcestershire sauce
1 tablespoon Dijon mustard
3 1/2 tablespoons lemon juice
1 1/2 ounces grated Parmesan cheese
1 tablespoon crushed garlic
Salt and black pepper to taste
2 heads romaine lettuce, cleaned, trimmed and chilled
Garlic Croutons (recipe next page)
Shredded Parmesan cheese for garnish

1. Mash cooked egg yolks into mustard, Worcestershire, lemon juice and red-wine vinegar. Add anchovies, garlic and grated Parmesan cheese. Slowly blend in olive oil, stirring constantly. Season to taste with salt and pepper.

2. In a large salad bowl, add romaine, torn or cut into bite size pieces; toss with dressing and garlic croutons. Garnish with shredded Parmesan.

Recipe notes: Traditional Caesar salads are made with raw egg yolks. Raw egg-linked salmonella poisoning can lead to unpleasant symptoms in healthy adults, including abdominal discomfort or fever. However, the symptoms could be life-threatening for infants, the elderly or people in weakened health due to past illness, surgery or impairment of the immune system.

Garlic Croutons

4 slices white bread, crusts trimmed
1 clove garlic, diced
4 tablespoons butter
Grated Parmesan cheese

1. Heat oven to 350 F.

2. Blend diced garlic into room-temperature butter. Spread on bread slices.

3. Cut bread into cubes and bake until cubes are toasty, stirring midway through baking. Remove from oven.

4. When almost but not entirely cool, sprinkle with grated Parmesan to taste. Toss with salad.

Brownie Banana Split Pizza

Yield: 10-12 servings

1 (15-ounce) package brownie mix
1 (8-ounce) package cream cheese, softened
1 (14-ounce) can sweetened condensed milk
   (not evaporated milk)
1/4 cup pineapple juice
1 teaspoon vanilla extract
2 tablespoons bottled lemon juice
Sliced bananas and strawberries
Pecan or walnut halves
1 (1-ounce) square semisweet chocolate
1 tablespoon margarine or butter

1. Heat oven to 350 F.

2. Prepare brownie mix as package directs. On greased pizza pan or baking sheet, press batter into 12-inch circle. Bake 15 to 20 minutes. Cool.

3. In a mixing bowl, beat cream cheese until fluffy. Gradually beat in sweetened condensed milk until smooth. Stir in pineapple juice and vanilla; chill thoroughly. Spoon filling over brownie crust.

4. Dip banana slices in bottled lemon juice; drain well. Arrange bananas, strawberries and nuts on top of cream cheese mixture.

5. In a small saucepan, over low heat, melt chocolate with margarine; drizzle over the top of fruit. Chill until set, about 1 hour. Refrigerate leftovers.

Thanksgiving

Menu
Honey Herb-Roasted Turkey, mashed potatoes, Marinated Brussel Sprouts,
Rum-Mango-Cranberry Relish, Pumpkin Pecan Pie (recipe page 105) or
Pumpkin Ice Cream Pie (recipe page 105)

Honey Herb-Roasted Turkey

Yield: 12 to 14 servings

1 stick butter, softened
1/4 cup finely chopped fresh herbs (sage,
   rose mary and thyme are a good combination)
2 tablespoons honey
12-to-14-pound turkey
Salt and pepper to taste

1. Heat oven to 350 F. Mix the butter, chopped herbs and honey together. Set aside.

2. Remove the giblets and neck from the body and neck cavities of the turkey, then rinse, drain and pat dry with clean paper towels.

3. Loosen the skin over the breasts by running your hands just under the skin. Try to reach with your fingers to also loosen the skin covering the legs. Set aside 2 tablespoons of the herb butter.

With clean, dry hands, rub the remaining herb butter under the skin, pushing it with your fingers over the legs.

4. Insert a meat thermometer into the thickest part of the breast muscle so the stem of the thermometer is parallel with the breastbone. If you prefer to use an instant-read thermometer, skip this step.

5. Rub the remaining 2 tablespoons of herb butter over the outside of the skin. Try to spread it evenly so the turkey will brown evenly. Season the turkey with salt and pepper. Place the turkey in the heated oven and roast for about 45 minutes, until it has turned a golden brown. Then tent the turkey with aluminum foil to keep it from getting too brown, and continue roasting. The total cooking time will be about 3 hours for a 12-pound turkey; check for doneness starting at 2 1/2 hours. The turkey is done when the thigh meat is 180 F, and the breast meat is 170 F.

Barney's Steakhouse's Marinated Brussels Sprouts

Yield: 12 to 14 servings

3 (10-ounce) packages frozen brussels sprouts
1 small onion, chopped
2 cloves of fresh garlic, minced
1/4 teaspoon thyme
1/4 teaspoon oregano
1 teaspoon monosodium glutamate (optional)
1 teaspoon chopped chives
1/3 cup sugar
1/2 teaspoon salt
1/4 teaspoon garlic powder
1/2 teaspoon freshly ground black pepper
1/4 cup tarragon vinegar
3/4 cup cider vinegar
1 1/2 cups salad oil
1 tablespoon dill

1. Blanch brussels sprouts briefly in boiling water for no more than 3 minutes, just long enough to thaw the sprouts. Do not let them become soft. The vegetables should be very crisp when marinated. Drain brussels sprouts thoroughly so that the water doesn't dilute the marinade.

2. Put remaining ingredients in a bowl and mix with a wire whisk. Combine marinade with brussels sprouts. Refrigerate vegetable mixture in a covered container overnight.

Rum-Mango-Cranberry Relish

Yield: 12 to 14 servings

2 cups fresh cranberries
1 cup water
2 ripe mangos, peeled and chopped, divided use
1/4 cup chopped mint
1/4 cup fresh lime juice
1 tablespoon orange-blossom honey
1/4 cup dark rum (or more to taste)

1. Pick over berries discarding any soft fruit. Put cranberries in a large saucepan. Add water and simmer until they pop, about 10 minutes.

2. Add to cranberries 1 chopped mango, mint, lime juice, honey and rum. Let mixture simmer over very low heat, stirring occasionally, until it thickens to desired consistency. Refrigerate for up to one day. Just before serving, stir in remaining chopped mango. Served chilled or at room temperature.

Recipe note: You can substitute 1 jar of mango spears (drained, rinsed and chopped) instead of fresh fruit.

Holiday Dinner Party

Menu
Brie Glazed with Kiwi and Cranberry Marmalade,
Herbed Beef Tenderloin, Garlic Roasted Vegetables,
mixed greens with dressing of choice
and Apple Cake (recipe page 100)

Brie Glazed With Kiwi and Cranberry Marmalade

Yield: 12 servings

1/2 cup dried cranberries
2 tablespoons currants
3 tablespoons dark brown sugar
1/8 teaspoon ground cloves
1/2 teaspoon minced fresh ginger
1/4 teaspoon ground allspice
1/4 teaspoon dry mustard
1/4 cup, plus 2 tablespoons water
2 kiwi, peeled, sliced, and quartered
2 tablespoons pecan pieces
1 wheel of brie cheese (about 1 pound)

1. Heat oven to 350 F.

2. Combine the cranberries, currants, brown sugar, cloves, ginger root, allspice, mustard and water in a medium saucepan. Cook gently over medium heat until mixture comes to a boil. Reduce heat to low and simmer until the cranberries swell and the liquid thickens into a jamlike consistency, about 8-10 minutes. Remove from heat and allow to cool completely. When cool, stir in the chopped pecan pieces.

3. Place the brie wheel on a parchment-lined cookie sheet. Spread the cooled cranberry marmalade evenly over the top of the brie. Bake for 25-30 minutes, or until the brie round swells. Remove from the oven and gently slide the brie onto a cheese board or plate. Top the cranberry marmalade with chopped kiwi.

4. Serve immediately with crisp crackers.

Herbed Beef Tenderloin With Garlic Roasted Vegetables

Yield: 8-10 servings

1 (4-pound) well-trimmed beef tenderloin roast
2 tablespoons grated Parmesan cheese
Seasoning:
1 teaspoon dried Italian seasoning
1/2 teaspoon cracked black pepper

1. Heat oven to 425 F.

2. Combine seasoning ingredients and press evenly into the roast.

3. Place beef on a rack in a shallow roasting pan. Insert a meat thermometer so bulb is centered in the thickest part. (Do not add water to cover.)

4. Roast 45-50 minutes for medium-rare to medium doneness. Remove the roast when thermometer registers 140 F for medium rare, 155 F for medium. Sprinkle cheese over the top. Let stand 15 minutes. Temperature will continue to rise to 145 F for medium rare, 160 F for medium as meat rests.

5. Carve roast into slices.

Garlic Roasted Vegetables

Yield: 8-10 servings

1 large head of garlic
3 medium-size potatoes, cut into quarters
4 small onions, cut in half
6 plum tomatoes, cut in half
2 medium zucchini, cut into 3/4-inch slices
1/4 cup freshly grated Parmesan cheese
Salt to taste
Seasoning:
2 tablespoons olive oil
1 teaspoon dried Italian seasoning
1/2 teaspoon cracked black pepper

1. Heat oven to 425 F.

2. Cut 1 inch off the top of the head of garlic, cutting through the tip of each clove. Discard top portion. Wrap garlic tightly in foil.

3. In a large bowl, combine seasoning ingredients. Add vegetables, tossing to coat. Remove tomatoes and zucchini from vegetable mixture and set aside.

4. Arrange potatoes, onions and foil-wrapped garlic on a 15-by-10-inch jellyroll pan. Roast with beef (see previous recipe) for 30 minutes.

5. Add tomatoes and zucchini to vegetables in jellyroll pan. Continue to roast 15 more minutes, or until all vegetables are tender.

6. Unwrap garlic. Squeeze softened cloves over vegetables. Top with Parmesan cheese and season with salt, if desired. Serve with Herbed Beef Tenderloin.

Kwanzaa

Menu
Caramelized Apple and Toasted Walnut Brie,
Rack of Pork With Parsleyed Crumbs, Rosemary Potatoes,
Key Lime Pie (recipe page 110)

The Kwanzaa table should be set with place mats to symbolize reverence for tradition, a large communal cup, an ear of dried corn for each child, a seven-branched candleholder, a bowl of fruit and vegetables, seven candles and gifts for children. The seven-day celebration starts on Dec. 26. Each night the household gathers to discuss one of the holiday's seven principles:

Umoja (unity): To strive for and maintain unity in family and community.

Kujichagulia (self-determination): To define oneself and one's life rather than having it defined by others.

Ujima (collective work and responsibility): To maintain the physical and spiritual community.

Ujamma (cooperative economics): To build and maintain shops and other businesses and to profit from them together.

Nia (purpose): To make the collective vocation the building of community.

Kuumba (creativity): To find ways to add beauty to the community.

Imani (faith): To believe in leaders and the righteousness of community struggle.

On the sixth night, New Year's Eve, a lavish feast called the Kwanzaa Karamu is set. The menu should be created from the cuisines of Africa, the Caribbean and South America.

Caramelized Apple and Toasted Walnut Brie

Yield: 8 appetizer servings

2 tablespoons butter
1 small red apple (such as Fuji or Braeburn),
 cored and sliced or chopped
1 tablespoon granulated sugar
15-ounce ripe, round brie, at room temperature
1/ 4 cup toasted, coarsely chopped walnuts

1. Melt butter in 10-inch nonstick skillet over medium heat. Add apple slices and sugar. Saute, tossing occasionally, until apples are soft and golden brown, about 12 minutes.

2. Let apple slices cool slightly. Carefully place chopped apple or fan apple slices over cheese; sprinkle with walnuts. May be served right away or chilled several hours. Serve at room temperature, accompanied with assorted crackers and bread slices.

Rack of Pork With Parsleyed Crumbs

Yield: 8 servings

1 whole rack of pork, backbone trimmed,
 about 7 or 8 ribs
Salt and coarsely ground black pepper, to taste
3/4 cup coarse-grained mustard
1 1/2 cups fresh bread crumbs
3/4 cup minced fresh parsley
1 tablespoon dried thyme, crumbled
3 garlic cloves, peeled and crushed

1. Heat oven to 350 F. Season pork with salt and pepper, as desired. Brush pork with 1/4 cup mustard.

2. In medium bowl, combine remaining mustard with remaining ingredients. Press crumb mixture evenly over top of pork.

3. Arrange rack of pork crumb side up in roasting pan. Roast for 1 1/2 hours, or until meat thermometer inserted into center of meaty part registers 155 F. Let rest 10 minutes. Carve pork, cutting between ribs, and serve.

Rosemary Potatoes

Yield: 6-8 servings

3 large baking potatoes
3 large sweet potatoes
Olive-oil flavored cooking spray
Olive oil
2 teaspoons minced garlic, or less to taste
2 tablespoons dried rosemary
Sprigs of fresh rosemary for garnish

1. Bake white and sweet potatoes in a conventional or microwave oven until tender. Let potatoes cool enough to handle. Cut potatoes into large chunks.

2. Heat oven to 350 F. Lightly coat a 9-by-13-inch baking pan with cooking spray. Place potatoes in pan.

3. Brush tops of potatoes with olive oil. Sprinkle garlic over potatoes. Stir potatoes with a wooden spoon to coat vegetables. Sprinkle dried rosemary over potatoes. Gently stir to coat.

4. Bake for 20 minutes, or until tops are crisp and potatoes are heated through. Serve garnished with fresh rosemary.

Menu suggestions for other celebrations

1. Derby Day Party
   Tarragon Shrimp and Orange Salad (page 42), Spiral Sandwiches (page 51), Mint Juleps (page 116), Run For the Roses Pie (page 104)

2. Mardi Gras
   Creamy Basil Dip (page 20), Cajun Pork Roast (page 52) or Jambalaya (page 57), coleslaw dressed with mint-flavored salad dressing, King Cake (page 92)

3. Rosh Hashanna
   Spicy White Bean Dip (page 25), Herbed Beef Tenderloin With Garlic Roasted Vegetables (page 87) Honey Almond Cheesecake (page 103) or Red Banana Brulee With Macaroon Crisp and Tangerine Salsa (page 101)

4. Graduation Party
   Harvey's Bistro's Smoked Shrimp and Artichoke Spread (page 19), Tex-Italian Pasta Fiesta (page 47) or Nature's Table Vegetarian Chili (page 48) and Cheesy Cornbread (page 48), Brownie Banana Split Pizza (page 81)

5. Basketball Playoff Party
   Bubbalou's Bodacious Bar-B-Q's Texas Caviar (page 18), Deli Roast Beef and Roasted Red Pepper Crostini (page 19), Muffuletta (page 45), Chocolate Chip Pecan Cookies (page 104)

6. Bowl Game Tailgate
   Black Bean Salsa (page 20), Artichoke Salad (page 37), Touchdown Beef and Honey Mustard Sandwich (page 50) or Honey-Mustard Glazed Chicken Wings With Green Onion-Sesame Confetti (page 56), Maple Pecan Oatmeal Bars (page 109)

7. Holiday Cookie Exchange Luncheon
   Sliced deli meats and assorted breads, condiments, Caesar Salad (page 80), Gingerbread Pudding Cake (page 93), Candy Cane Cookies to exchange with guests (page 100)

8. Apres Theater/Concert Gathering
   Regular and decaf coffee, hot tea, Sour Cream Peach Mince Pie (page 94), Glazed Pecans (page 52).

Festive Treats & Desserts

King Cake

Twelfth Night dinners or Feasts of the Epiphany signal the end of the holiday season.
These gatherings also mark the beginning of Mardi Gras season, which will culminate on the day before Lent.
Yield: 24 servings

For the cake:
1/2 cup butter
1/2 cup milk
1/2 cup sugar
1/2 teaspoon salt
1/3 cup warm water
2 packages dry active yeast
3 large eggs, beaten
1 teaspoon freshly grated lemon zest
1 teaspoon freshly grated orange zest
1 teaspoon ground nutmeg
1 teaspoon cinnamon (optional)
4 to 5 cups all-purpose flour
1/4 cup granulated sugar mixed with cinnamon to
   taste
Small token or bean
For the icing:
1 1/2 cups powdered sugar
1 tablespoon water
2 tablespoons dark rum
1 teaspoon freshly squeezed lemon juice
Yellow, green and purple cake-decorating
   sugars

No time to cook? These Louisiana bakeries will do the work for
you:
—Gambino's, 1-800-426-2466.
—Haydel's Bakery, 1-800-442-1342.

1. Combine butter, sugar, milk and salt. Stir over medium heat until the butter melts and mixture is steaming. Remove from heat; let mixture cool.

2. Pour the warm water into a large bowl. Sprinkle the yeast on top. Swirl the bowl to allow yeast to dissolve. The mixture will become slightly frothy. Pour the warm milk mixture into yeast (if it is too hot it will kill the yeast). Stir in the beaten eggs, lemon and orange zest, nutmeg, 1 teaspoon of cinnamon and 2 cups of the flour. Stir until free of lumps. Add 2 more cups of flour and stir until the dough holds together and is easy to handle.

3. Turn dough out on a lightly floured board. Knead for 5 minutes, adding flour as necessary to make a springy dough. Wash and grease mixing bowl. Add the dough and roll it so all surfaces are covered lightly with grease. Cover the bowl with a cloth and allow dough to rise for 2 hours or until it doubles in volume.

4. Punch dough down and divide into 3 equal parts. Roll each part into a rope about 30 inches long. Press a small token or bean, into one of the strands of dough.

5. Sprinkle the cinnamon-flavored sugar on the work surface. Roll the long strands of dough in the mixture to coat the dough. Carefully braid the strands of dough to form a thick braid. Twist the braid together to make a large ring shape and pinch the ends together to seal. Cover the ring loosely with plastic wrap and let dough rise for 1 hour.

6. Heat the oven to 375 F. Bake cake for 15 to 20 minutes or until surface is golden brown. Remove from oven and cool.

7. Mix together powdered sugar, rum, water and lemon juice to make the icing. Drizzle icing over cooled cake. Sprinkle icing with yellow, green and purple cake-decorating sugars.

Recipe notes: Colored cake-decorating sugars are available in cake-decorating shops. The texture of this cake is similar to challah bread.

Gingerbread Pudding Cake

Old-Fashioned Pudding Cake makes a comeback in this warm gingerbread dessert.
Yield: 12 servings

2 1/2 cups all-purpose flour
1 1/2 teaspoons baking soda
1 1/4 teaspoons ground ginger
1 teaspoon cinnamon
1/2 teaspoon salt
1/2 teaspoon ground allspice
1/2 teaspoon ground nutmeg
1/2 cup butter, softened
1/2 cup sugar
1 egg
1 cup molasses
1 cup water
3/4 cup firmly packed brown sugar
1/3 cup butter, melted
1 1/2 cups hot water
Pumpkin-flavored ice cream (see note)

1. Heat oven to 350 F.

2. Combine flour, soda, ginger, cinnamon, salt, allspice and nutmeg; set aside.

3. In a large mixer bowl, beat 1/2 cup butter and sugar on medium speed until creamy (1-2 minutes). Add egg; continue beating until well mixed. Reduce speed to low. Continue beating, alternately adding flour mixture with molasses and 1 cup water, beating after each addition only until blended.

4. Pour batter into 13-by-9-inch baking pan. Sprinkle batter with 3/4 cup brown sugar.

5. Combine 1/3 cup melted butter and 1 1/2 cups hot water; carefully pour on top of batter. Bake for 40-55 minutes or until gingerbread is cracked on top and toothpick inserted in center comes out clean. Serve warm with pumpkin-flavored ice cream.

Recipe note: If you can't find prepared pumpkin-flavored ice cream in the supermarket, stir in canned pumpkin to taste into good quality vanilla ice cream. Add some pumpkin pie spice if desired.

Sour Cream Peach Mince Pie

Yield: 8 to 10 servings

1 (15-16-ounce) can sliced peaches, well-drained
1 (9-inch) unbaked pastry shell
1 (27-ounce) jar ready-to-use mincemeat (regular
   or brandy and rum)
1 1/2 cups sour cream
1/4 cup confectioners' sugar

Recipe note: You can substitute 1 (9-ounce) package condensed mincemeat, reconstituted according to package directions, for ready-to-use mincemeat.

1. Place rack in lowest position in oven. Heat oven to 400 F.

2. Reserve 3 peach slices, slicing each in half to make 6 slices; set aside. Chop remaining peaches and put on the bottom of pastry shell. Top with mincemeat. Bake 20 minutes. Remove from oven.

3. Combine sour cream and sugar. Spread over top of pie and bake 10 more minutes.

4. Cool pie, then chill thoroughly. Garnish with reserved peach slices.

Blueberry and Custard-Filled Star Puffs

Yield: 6 servings

1 sheet (from a 17-ounce package) frozen puff
   pastry, thawed
1 (3 3/8 -ounce) package instant vanilla pudding
   and pie filling
1 cup milk
1 (8-ounce) container sour cream
1 pint (about 2 cups) fresh blueberries
1 tablespoon sugar
1 tablespoon chopped fresh mint (optional)
1/2 teaspoon grated orange peel
Confectioners' sugar

1. Heat oven to 400 F. Unfold puff pastry. With a rolling pin, roll pastry out 1/2 inch wider than its dimensions. Using a 3-inch, star-shaped cookie cutter, cut out 12 stars. Transfer stars onto an ungreased baking sheet 1 inch apart.

2. Bake until puffed and golden, about 15 minutes. Transfer stars onto a wire rack. Cool slightly. Using a knife, cut stars in half horizontally. Cool completely.

3. Combine pudding mix and milk. Using a mixer, beat until mixture is smooth, about 2 minutes. Fold in sour cream. Refrigerate, covered, until thickened, about 15 minutes.

4. Combine blueberries, sugar, mint and orange peel. Refrigerate, covered, until ready to serve.

Using a strainer, sprinkle tops of stars with confectioners' sugar. Set aside. On each plate, place 2 star bottoms; spoon 1/3 cup sauce and 1/3 cup blueberries onto bottoms. Top with reserved star tops.

Recipe note: Add strawberries or carambola (star fruit) to the blueberry mixture for a Fourth of July or New Year's Eve get-together.

White Chocolate Berry Pie

Yield: 10-12 servings

1 (9-inch) baked pastry shell, cooled
5 squares Baker's premium white baking chocolate (see note)
2 tablespoons milk (see note)
4 ounces Philadelphia Brand cream cheese, softened
1/3 cup powdered sugar
1 teaspoon grated orange peel
1 cup whipping cream, whipped
1 pint raspberries or strawberries
1 square Baker's premium white baking chocolate, melted

1. Microwave 5 squares white chocolate and milk in large microwavable bowl on high (100 percent power) for 2 minutes or until chocolate is almost melted, stirring halfway through heating time. Stir until chocolate is completely melted. Cool to room temperature.

2. Beat cream cheese, powdered sugar and orange peel in small bowl with mixer on low speed until smooth. Beat into chocolate mixture.

3. Fold whipped cream into chocolate mixture. Spread in bottom of pastry shell. Place raspberries on filling. Drizzle with melted chocolate.

4. Refrigerate 1 hour or until ready to serve.

Recipe note: Or use 1 (4-ounce) package Baker's German's sweet chocolate bar or 4 squares Baker's semisweet baking chocolate and 1/4 cup milk.

Mocha Drizzle

Yield: 4 servings

1 (3-ounce) package ladyfingers
1 1/2 teaspoons cornstarch
2 1/2 teaspoons instant coffee granules
4 teaspoons sugar
1/2 cup water, plus 3 tablespoons, divided use
12 ounces frozen light whipped dessert topping, thawed
1 pint chocolate nonfat frozen yogurt
Vegetable cooking spray

1. Heat oven to 400 F.

2. Spray the insides of four custard cups (3/4 cup size) with cooking spray. Stand 5 ladyfinger halves in each cup with the split surface upward. The ladyfingers should be evenly spaced and overlap in the center. They may extend slightly above the tops of the cups. Where the cookies overlap, press them firmly together.

3. Bake for 4-6 minutes until golden brown and crisp. Cool completely. Wrap remaining ladyfingers in plastic food wrap and store in the freezer for another use.

4. To make the coffee syrup, whisk cornstarch, coffee, sugar and 1/2 cup water together. Microwave on high (100 percent) power for 1-1 1/2 minutes until boiling rapidly, stirring once. Cool to room temperature (do not refrigerate).

5. Whisk half of the whipped topping with 3 tablespoons of water to make a vanilla sauce. Cover and refrigerate.

6. Divide the vanilla sauce among 4 plates. Using a flexible spatula, loosen ladyfinger cups from the bottoms of the custard cups; do not remove.

7. Using a 1/4 cup ice cream scoop, scoop a small ball of frozen yogurt into each cup. Carefully put the filled cups on the plates. Drizzle 2 tablespoons of the coffee syrup over each cup. Add a dab of remaining whipped topping to each.

Straub's Boatyard's Foster Sauce

This indulgent sauce can be served over ice cream, poundcake, frozen yogurt or puff pastry.
Yield: 16 servings

2 sticks sweet butter
1 pound light brown sugar
3 tablespoons Grand Marnier
1 cup heavy whipping cream

1. In a saucepan, combine butter and brown sugar over high heat. Bring mixture to a rolling boil, stirring to make sure sugar is completely dissolved.

2. Remove pan from heat and immediately add the Grand Marnier and heavy cream. Stir to blend well.

3. Let mixture cool. Serve over poundcake. Refrigerate unused sauce.

No-fuss Desserts

-Top ice cream with pureed fruit sauces - raspberries, blackberries and strawberries are especially good. They can be enhanced with a dash of liqueur, if desired.

-Arrange a selection of cheeses with apple slices and seedless grapes on a large platter and let dinner guests serve themselves.

-Jazz up store-bought cakes by placing slices in a pool of store-bought sauce. Add a touch of liqueur, if desired.

-Place a basket of gourmet cookies in the center of the buffet or dinner table and let guests help themselves.

-Sprinkle berries with champagne, cognac, kirsch or orange liqueur and serve them with shortbread.

-Prepare a packaged brownie mix in a round pan and layer with whipped cream and strawberry slices.

Apple Cake

This cake is one of the most popular dessert selections of Fenwick Catering in Orlando.
The joy of it all is its outrageous simplicity.
Yield: 16 servings

3 to 4 Granny Smith apples
1 (18.5-ounce) box Duncan Hines Yellow
　Cake Mix
1 part cinnamon to 3 parts sugar for topping
1 (10-by-14-inch) cake pan

1. Heat oven to 350 F.

2. Peel, core and slice apples; set aside. Following directions on back of cake box mix batter.

3. Pour cake batter into greased pan. Line sliced apples in rows on top of batter. Sprinkle top of cake with cinnamon-sugar. Place in the oven for about 30 minutes or until golden brown. Test with pick to be sure cake is done in center.

Candy Cane Cookies

Keep the dough for these cookies well-chilled while you are rolling the strips.
Take the baked candy canes to a cookie exchange or serve them at a holiday caroling party.
Yield: 2 dozen

1 cup unsalted butter
1 cup sifted confectioners' sugar
1 large egg
1/2 teaspoon vanilla extract
1/2 teaspoon peppermint extract
1/4 teaspoon salt
2 1/2 cups sifted all-purpose flour
1/4 teaspoon red food coloring

1. Blend butter with confectioners' sugar until fluffy. Beat in egg, extracts, salt, flour. Divide in half. Stir food coloring into 1 piece. Refrigerate doughs for several hours.

2. Heat oven to 350 F. Shape teaspoon of plain dough into 4-inch cylinder. Do same with red dough. Twist together. Bend into a cane shape. Put 1-2 inches apart on a baking sheet. Bake 8-10 minutes. Do not allow to brown.

Red Banana Brulee With Macaroon Crisp and Tangerine Salsa

This recipe was developed by chef Allan Susser of Aventura, Fla.
The salsa filling can be used as a sauce for frozen yogurt.
Yield: 6 servings

6 sprigs of mint for garnish
Tangerine salsa:
3 tangerines
2 medium-size oranges
1 medium mango
2 tablespoons honey
3 tablespoons brewed orange pekoe tea
2 tablespoons toasted almonds
Macaroons:
2 cups almond paste
1 cup granulated sugar
2 large egg whites
Red banana brulee:
6 medium-ripe bananas
1 tablespoons freshly squeezed lime juice
1/4 teaspoon vanilla extract
3 tablespoons light brown sugar

1. To prepare the salsa, peel tangerines and oranges. Cut membranes to remove the segments and seeds. Cut the segments into thirds and place them in a mixing bowl. Peel mango, remove seed and dice fruit. Add diced mango to mixing bowl. Add the honey, tea and almonds. Mix well and chill.

2. To make macaroons, heat oven to 350 F. With a wooden spoon, combine the almond paste, sugar and egg whites in a stainless-steel bowl. Line a cookie sheet with parchment paper. Spoon out the macaroon mixture and press out the size of a 2-by-6-inch oval (about 1/3 inch thick). Bake macaroons for 15 minutes, until the edges are golden brown. Remove from the oven and allow to cool.

3. To make brulee, peel the bananas. Split bananas in half and place them in a flat glass dish, cut side up. Combine lime juice and vanilla. Brush bananas with the lime juice mixture. Spoon the brown sugar on the bananas. Heat the broiler to very hot. Place the sugar-topped bananas under the broiler for 2-3 minutes. Remove pan from the broiler and let them cool for 1 minute before removing from the pan. Transfer the cooked banana to the macaroon crisps and pour remaining juices over the top of each.

4. Into small colorful oval bowls divide the tangerine salsa. Place one of the brulee-filled macaroon crisps into each bowl. Garnish with fresh mint.

Honey-Almond Cheesecake

Matzo meal and honey combine to make the crust for this delicious cheesecake.
Yield: 10 servings

Matzo meal crust:
1 cup matzo meal
1/3 cup softened butter
1/3 cup water
1 tablespoon honey
Filling:
1 pound low-fat cream cheese, softened
2/3 cup honey
5 eggs, separated
2 cups low-fat sour cream, divided
2 teaspoons vanilla extract, divided
1/2 teaspoon almond extract
1/2 cup cake flour
Sliced kiwis for garnish
Sliced strawberries for garnish

1. Heat oven to 350 F. Process matzo meal in the work bowl of a food processor until texture is very fine. Cut in softened butter until mixture resembles coarse meal. Combine water and 1 tablespoon of honey. Sprinkle over matzo mixture. Mix lightly. Press into the bottom of a 9-inch springform pan with a removable bottom. Bake for 12 minutes or until edges brown. Cool completely.

2. Lower oven temperature to 300 F. Beat cream cheese and 2/3 cup honey until smooth and fluffy. Add the egg yolks, one at a time, beating after each addition. At low speed, beat in 1 cup of the sour cream, 1 teaspoon of vanilla extract and almond extract. Stir in flour.

3. Beat egg whites until stiff. Gently fold whites by thirds into the honey-cream cheese mixture. Pour batter into the cooled crust. Bake 1 hour, or until set. Some ovens may require an additional 30 minutes for cheesecake to set.) Cool to room temperature on a rack. Refrigerate at least 2 hours.

4. Combine remaining 1 cup sour cream and teaspoon of vanilla. Carefully spread over cooled cheesecake. Refrigerate for an additional hour. Remove sides of pan and garnish with sliced kiwi and strawberries.

Run For the Roses Pie

This bourbon-flavored pie is a favorite for Kentucky Derby parties.
Yield: 8-10 servings

1 cup granulated sugar
1/2 cup all purpose flour
1/2 cup butter or margarine, melted and slightly
   cooled
2 eggs, slightly beaten
2 tablespoons bourbon
1 teaspoon vanilla extract
1 cup semisweet chocolate morsels
1 cup chopped pecans or walnuts
1 (9-or-10-inch) deep pie shell, unbaked

1. Heat oven to 325F.

2. Combine sugar, flour, butter, eggs, bourbon and vanilla in a mixer bowl, beating until well-blended. Stir in chocolate morsels and nuts. Spoon mixture into pie shell.

3. Bake for 50 minutes to 1 hour, or until pie is set and top cracks. Cool on rack.

Chocolate Chip Pecan Cookies

Yield: about 112 cookies

2 cups butter
2 cups light brown sugar
2 cups sugar
4 eggs
2 teaspoons vanilla
4 cups flour
5 cups blended oatmeal (see note)
1 teaspoon salt
2 teaspoons baking powder
2 teaspoons baking soda
24 ounces chocolate chips
1 (8-ounce) Hershey Bar, grated
3 cups chopped pecans

1. Heat oven to 375F.

2. Blend together butter and both sugars. Add eggs and vanilla. Mix in flour, blended oatmeal, salt, baking powder and baking soda. Add chocolate chips, grated Hershey bar and nuts.

3. Roll into balls and place 2 inches apart on a cookie sheet. Bake for 10 minutes.

Recipe note: To make blended oatmeal, put oatmeal into the work bowl of a blender and process to a fine powder.

Pumpkin Pecan Pie

Yield: 8 servings

1 (9-inch) unbaked pie shell
Pumpkin layer:
1 cup solid-pack pumpkin
1/3 cup granulated sugar
1 egg
1 teaspoon pumpkin pie spice
Pecan layer:
2/3 cup light corn syrup
1/2 cup granulated sugar
2 eggs
3 tablespoons butter or margarine, melted
1/2 teaspoon vanilla extract
1 cup pecan halves

1. Heat oven to 350 F.

2. Combine pumpkin layer ingredients. Spread over bottom of shell. Combine corn syrup, sugar, eggs, butter and vanilla. Stir in nuts. Spoon over pumpkin mixture.

3. Bake 50 minutes or until a knife inserted in the center comes out clean.

Pumpkin Ice Cream Pie

This freezer pie is easy to make. For a peppery contrast to the smooth and creamy filling, make a gingersnap crust.
Yield: 6-8 servings

1 pint vanilla ice cream, softened
1 (9-inch) graham cracker pie crust
1 cup canned solid-pack pumpkin
3/4 cup sugar
1/2 teaspoon ground ginger
1/2 teaspoon cinnamon
1/2 teaspoon salt
1/4 teaspoon nutmeg
1 cup whipping cream

1. Spoon ice cream into pie crust. Freeze while preparing pumpkin layer.

2. Combine pumpkin, sugar, ginger, cinnamon, salt and nutmeg. Whip cream to stiff peaks. Fold pumpkin mixture into whipped cream.

3. Remove pie crust from freezer. Spread pumpkin mixture evenly over ice cream. Cover and freeze for at least 8 hours or overnight. Serve frozen.

Strawberry Cream Dip for Fruit

Yield: 4 servings

1/2 cup light sour cream
1/4 cup strawberry fruit spread (no sugar added)
Washed strawberries and banana pieces for
   dipping

1. In a small bowl, combine all ingredients.

2. Cover and chill for at least 1 hour before serving with fruit.

Chocolate Fudge Dip

Yield: 4 servings

6 tablespoons plain nonfat yogurt
6 tablespoons prepared nonfat chocolate
   fudge sauce
1 1/2 teaspoons frozen orange juice concentrate,
   thawed
Washed strawberries and banana pieces for
   dipping

1. In a small bowl, combine all ingredients.

2. Cover and chill for at least 1 hour before serving with fruit.

Honey Almond Dip

Yield: 4 servings

2/3 cup plain nonfat yogurt
3 tablespoons toasted, slivered almonds, finely
   chopped
2 1/2 tablespoons honey
Washed strawberries for dipping

1. In a small bowl, combine all ingredients.

2. Cover and chill for at least 1 hour before serving with fruit.

Maple Pecan Oatmeal Bars

Make these bars for weekend picnics or snacks for a teen slumber party.
Yield: 32 bars

1/3 cup maple flavored pancake syrup
3/4 cup (1 1/2 sticks) butter or margarine
2 1/4 cups quick or old-fashioned oats,
   uncooked
2 cups all-purpose flour
1 1/2 cups firmly packed brown sugar
3/4 cup shredded coconut (optional)
1 teaspoon baking soda
1/4 teaspoon salt (optional)
1 egg, lightly beaten
1 teaspoon vanilla
Topping:
1 1/2 cups chopped pecans (about 6 ounces)
1/4 cup firmly packed brown sugar
1/3 cup maple flavored pancake syrup

1. Heat oven to 350 F. Lightly spray 13 x 9-inch baking pan with cooking spray.

2. For the bars, melt butter; set aside to cool. In large bowl, combine oats, flour, brown sugar, coconut, baking soda and salt; mix well. In small bowl, combine melted butter, syrup, egg and vanilla; mix well. Add to oat mixture; mix well. Dough will be stiff. Press dough evenly onto bottom of pan.

3. For topping, combine pecans and brown sugar in small bowl. Sprinkle evenly over dough; press down lightly. Drizzle syrup evenly over pecans. Bake 35 to 38 minutes or until edges are set but middle is soft. (Do not overbake.) Cool completely in pan on wire rack. Cut into bars. Store tightly covered.

Key Lime Pie

Yield: 8-10 servings

3 to 4 egg yolks
1 (14-ounce) can sweetened condensed milk (not
  evaporated)
1/2 cup fresh Key lime juice
1 (9-inch) graham cracker crust
Whipped cream (optional)

1. Heat oven to 350 F.

2. Beat the egg yolks slightly, then stir in the condensed milk and lime juice. The mixture should thicken a bit after 2 or 3 minutes of stirring. Pour into crust.

3. Bake 15 minutcs, or until set. Chill pie overnight. Top with whipped cream, if desired.

Recipe notes: For a dramatic presentation, make a thick paste with graham cracker crumbs, melted butter and a drop or two of water. With a wooden ice cream stick, add the paste to the rim of the slightly cooled, baked pie. When pie chills, the decorative rim will become firm.

Chocolate Dipped Delights

*These dipped treats are great for serving at brunches, showers or afternoon teas.
Keep them in mind for gift-giving as well.*
Yield: about 2 dozen candies

1 package sweet cooking chocolate bar, semisweet
  chocolate squares or white baking chocolate squares
Assorted dippers such as peppermint sticks, dried
  apricots and pretzels

1. In a microwave, melt chocolate on high (100 percent power) for 2 minutes, stirring halfway through cooking time.

2. Dip dippers into chocolate, letting excess drip off. Refrigerate on wax paper-lined tray for 30 minutes.

Desserts without the guilt

-Make heart-shaped meringue shells and serve with fresh strawberries and a drizzle of Grand Marnier.

-Bake squares of phyllo dough in regular-or jumbo-size muffin tins, cool, and fill with low-fat vanilla pudding and raspberries.

-Serve slices of angel food cake with a brandy sauce or coffee liqueur.

-Create an elegant parfait with frozen yogurt (flavor of your choice) and slices of kiwi fruit. Top each serving with a tablespoon of all-fruit spread, if desired.

-Cut a good-size orange in half and remove fruit. Mash fruit into vanilla frozen yogurt. Put yogurt mixture into orange halves to mold. Freeze for at least 2 hours or overnight. Unmold onto dessert plates and serve with a sprig of fresh mint.

Entertaining tip

If you want to liven up your dinner party plates, try presenting sauces in interesting patterns. Swirled sauces look difficult but are quite easy. You make a puddle of one sauce, use a ketchup bottle to add circles or spirals with a contrasting sauce, then draw a knife through the two to create a squiggle pattern.

Festive Beverages

Marriott's Orlando World Center's Rum Runner

Yield: 1 serving

1 ounce Bacardi Light Rum
1/2 ounce blackberry brandy
1/2 ounce creme de banana
3 ounces fresh orange juice
3 ounces pineapple juice
Dash cherry juice
1/2 ounce Bacardi Black Rum
Fruits of choice for garnish

1. Combine light rum, brandy, creme de banana and fruit juices. Shake and strain over ice.

2. Top with 1/2 ounce Bacardi Black rum and garnish.

Disney's Yacht & Beach Club Resort's Hurricane

Yield: 1 serving

1 ounce Myers's Rum
3/4 ounce peach schnapps
3 ounces orange juice
Splash grenadine
1/2 ounce Bacardi 151 Rum
Cherry and orange slice for garnish

1. Fill hurricane glass with ice.

2. Combine Myers's rum, schnapps, orange juice and grenadine. Pour over ice. Top off with Bacardi 151 rum. Garnish with cherry and orange slice.

The Langford Resort Hotel's Tropical Punch

Yield: 1 serving

1/2 ounce lemon juice
Ice
1 1/2 ounces white rum
1 1/2 ounces Myers's Dark Rum
2 ounces orange juice
2 ounces pineapple juice
Slice of orange and maraschino cherry for garnish

1. Put lemon juice in the bottom of a tall glass.

2. Add rums and fruit juices. Shake and strain over ice.

3. Garnish with an orange slice and cherry.

Hyatt Regency Grand Cypress' Papa Doble from Hemingway's

Yield: 1 serving

1 1/4 ounces Bacardi White Rum
1 1/2 ounces Captain Morgan Spiced Rum
Juice of half a lime
Equal portions of pineapple, orange and grapefruit
  juice to taste
6 drops of maraschino cherry juice

1. Combine rums and fruit juices with 6 drops of maraschino cherry juice.

2. Shake and strain over ice. Serve.

Fresh Fruit Daiquiris

Substitute peaches, bananas or any other sweet fruit for the berries in this recipe.
Simply omit the rum to make "virgin" daiquiris.
Yield: 6 servings

9 ounces rum
4 ounces lime juice
2 tablespoons confectioners' sugar
8 ounces frozen strawberries or
    raspberries
2 to 3 cups crushed ice

1. In a blender, gently mix the rum, lime juice and sugar. Add the berries and ice and blend on high.

2. Serve in a chilled glass.

Margaritas

Margaritas are the third most popular drink prepared at home.
Yield: 6 servings

9 ounces tequila
3 ounces triple sec
6 ounces lemon or lime juice

1. Rub rims of cocktail glasses with rind of lemon or lime, dip rims in salt.

2. Shake ingredients with ice and strain into salt-rimmed glasses.

The Peabody Hotel's Mint Julep

A Derby Day party wouldn't be complete without this beverage.
Yield: 1 serving

3 mint leaves
2 teaspoons superfine sugar
2 ounces bourbon
Ice
3 1/2 ounces water
Additional mint for garnish

1. Muddle mint leaves in the bottom of a glass until mixture is pasty. (Muddle means to mash or crush ingredients with a spoon or a muddler - a rod with a flattened end.)

2. Combine sugar with mint mixture.

3. Pull out spoon or muddler and gently press it against the rim of glass to add flavor and aroma. Add bourbon. Fill glass with ice and finish with water. Mix well. Garnish with mint.

Real Irish Coffee

For an Irishman coming to the United States, it's quite a shock to see what passes as Irish coffee. Chef Patrick Reilly, a native of Ireland and chef/owner at Cafe Citron in Longwood, Fla., says he's convinced it is a mortal sin to use canned whipped cream. And as for creme de menthe? "Don't even think about it."
Yield: 1 serving

2 teaspoons brown sugar
Fresh brewed coffee
1 ounce Jameson or Powers Irish whiskey
1/4 cup heavy cream

1. Wash a small water glass or a wine glass with hot water, rinse well and dry.

2. Place two teaspoons of brown sugar in the glass, then fill with fresh, brewed coffee to within 1 inch of the rim. Stir thoroughly to dissolve the sugar.

3. Pour in about an ounce of Jameson or Powers Irish whiskey.

4. Slightly whip heavy cream with a whisk, only long enough so that it thickens a bit. Then pour the cream gently into the glass, pouring it over the back of a teaspoon until the cream forms a gentle "head" on the coffee. Refrigerate unused cream.

Minted Citrus Punch

The great thing about punches is that there are no rules.
Taste as you combine the ingredients and adjust the flavorings as you wish.
Yield: 20 servings

2 (6-ounce) cans frozen orange juice concentrate
1 (6-ounce) can frozen lemonade concentrate
1/2 teaspoon mint extract
6 cups cold water
3 1/2 cups club soda (see note)
1 large orange, cut into thin rounds (you should have at least 10 slices)
Small mint leaves for garnish

1. In a pitcher, combine concentrates, extract and cold water. When concentrates are dissolved, slowly pour juice mixture into a large punch bowl.

2. Add the club soda in 1 cup increments, tasting as you add. (Two cups of club soda will create a fruity punch with minimal fizz. Three and a half cups will create a lighter libation.

3. Float orange slices in punch bowl, topping each slice with a small mint leaf.

White Sangria

Sangria is an inexpensive, flavorful Spanish concoction.
Most people are familiar with red sangrias, but white sangrias are just as refreshing.
Yield: 4 servings

1 large orange
1 lemon, cut into thin slices
1 bottle dry white wine (see note)
2 tablespoons extra-fine sugar (see note)
1 ounce brandy
1 ounce Cointreau
2 cups ice cubes
1 cup club soda
Sliced carambola (star fruit) for garnish (optional)

1. Cut the orange in half. Cut one of the orange halves into thin slices. Juice the other orange half.

2. In a clear glass pitcher, combine the orange and lemon slices, orange juice, white wine, sugar, brandy and Cointreau. Chill pitcher for at least one hour to allow the flavors to meld.

3. When ready to serve, stir in ice cubes and club soda. Pour into wine goblets or glass tumblers. Float carambola slice on the top of each serving.

Recipe notes: To make a red sangria, substitute a bottle of dry red wine.
Extra-fine sugar dissolves faster in beverages than granulated sugar. You can make your own by grinding a few cups of regular sugar in the work bowl of a food processor.

Christmas Punch

This recipe makes an elegant addition to a holiday buffet.
The cranberry garnish adds a festive splash of color.
Yield: 20 servings

1 cup frozen orange juice
1 cup frozen lemonade
1 cup pineapple juice
2 quarts ginger ale
2 1/2 pints water
Vodka to taste
1/2 cup fresh cranberries for garnish

1. Combine all ingredients in the punch bowl. Garnish with half of the cranberries, reserving the remaining berries to refresh the punch during the party.

Citrus Kickoff Punch

This is a great beverage for winter football-watching parties.
Yield: 10 1/2 cups

1 orange, unpeeled, cut in half slices
1 lemon, unpeeled, cut in half slices
1/2 cup sugar
1 (10-ounce) package strawberries with sugar, partially thawed.
1 bottle ginger ale, chilled
1 (1-liter) bottle chablis, white zinfandel or Rhine wine, chilled
1 cup fresh lemon juice

1. Place citrus slices in a bowl with sugar. Using the back of a wooden spoon, crush fruit slightly to extract some juice. Add strawberries. Chill mixture for at least 1 hour.

2. To serve, pour fruit mixture over a small block of ice in a punch bowl. Stir in remaining ingredients.

How to make traditional cocktails

Dry martini: Pour 1 2/3 ounces gin and 1/3 ounce dry vermouth over ice cubes in a mixing glass, then strain into a cocktail glass. Serve with a twist of lemon peel or olive, if desired.

Gimlet: Pour 1 ounce lime juice, 1 teaspoon powdered sugar, 1 1/2 ounces gin over ice cubes in a mixing glass, then strain into a cocktail glass.

Kir Royale: Serve 6 ounces sparkling wine with a splash of Creme de Cassis in a large sparkling wine glass.

Manhattan: Stir 3/4 ounce sweet vermouth and 1 1/2 ounces blended whiskey with ice, strain into a cocktail glass and serve with a cherry.

Rob Roy: Stir 3/4 ounce sweet vermouth and 1 1/2 ounces scotch with ice and strain into a cocktail glass.

Singapore Sling: Shake juice of 1/2 lemon, 1 teaspoon powdered sugar and 2 ounces gin with ice, strain into a tall glass over ice cubes. Top with carbonated water and maraschino cherry, with 1/4 ounce cherry flavored brandy on top.

Stinger: Shake 1/2 ounce white Creme de Menthe and 1 1/2 ounces brandy with ice and strain into a cocktail glass.

Tom Collins: Shake juice of 1/2 lemon, 1 teaspoon powdered sugar and 2 ounces gin with ice, strain into a tall glass over several ice cubes. Top off with carbonated water and garnish with citrus slices and a maraschino cherry.

SOURCE: *Mr. Boston's Official Bartenders Guide*

What to buy

There is no standard shopping list for alcohol at small cocktail parties because most people are familiar with what their friends like to drink. But if you're not sure about beverage preferences, be sure to have the bar stocked with bourbon, rum, scotch, gin, white and red wine. Also have plenty of nonalcoholic alternatives and mixers available - tonic water, cranberry juice, orange juice, club soda and colas. Sparkling waters often come in snazzy bottles that will add color to the bar.

Party essentials

Glassware (3 glasses per guest)	Cocktail strainer
Ice bucket and tongs	Rod or long bar spoon
Cocktail shaker	Corkscrew
Martini pitcher	Jigger

How to plan for cocktails

For 4 guests: Lunch, 6 drinks; cocktails, 8; dinner, 8; for a whole evening: 16.
For 6 guests: Lunch, 10; cocktails, 12; dinner, 12; for a whole evening, 24.
For 10 guests: Lunch, 15; cocktails, 20; dinner, 20; for a whole evening, 40.

How many drinks per bottle

For cocktails, mixed drinks, based on 1.5-ounce liquor servings

1 bottle yields:
750 ml - 16 drinks
Liter - 22
1.5 liter - 39

4 bottles yield:
750 ml - 67
Liter - 90
1.5 liter - 157

8 bottles yield
750 ml - 135
Liter - 180
1.5 liter - 315

2 bottles yield:
750 ml - 33
Liter - 45
1.5 liter - 78

6 bottles yield:
750 ml - 101
Liter - 135
1.5 liter - 236

Glassware tips

Avoid plastic cups. The clinking of ice on glass is essential to the cocktail party ambience.

Six-ounce glasses are suitable for on-the-rocks drinks, and 3-ounce stemmed martini glasses are a must-have for gin and vermouth concoctions. Tall Collins glasses are optional, but if you do splurge for them, they can double as ice tea vessels after the party.

Special Helps & Entertaining Tips

Funky serving dishes

If you are shopping for serving pieces for outdoor gatherings, don't overlook garden shops. Yes, garden shops.

Just a couple of aisles away from fertilizers, insecticides and bags of peat moss are shelves with rows and rows of pots and trays that make creative serving pieces for foods.

It's important not to utilize old, used pots for food. Some plants and soils are treated with fertilizers and other substances meant for plant critters, not your dinner guests.

Here are some serving suggestions:

Use new, lined terra cotta drain plates for flat platters. Crisp garden vegetables look perfectly at home on these round plates.

Line small pots with plastic wrap or aluminum foil and fill with vegetable sticks and dip. For dips, insert a disposable plastic cup that has been lopped off to fit the height of the pot. This will help keep the food safe and keep oily concoctions from seeping into the porous terra cotta walls.

Fill a new faux stone pedestal planter with sangria or punch. (Look for vessels made from hard plastic material and remember to plug the drain hole.)

Place a small wood planter box on the buffet table and fill it with condiment bottles or paper plates and disposable cutlery.

Fill a large garden tub or plastic wheelbarrow with ice to keep wine, beer and soft drinks chilled. Tie ribbons or bandanas around the handles for a decorative touch.

Centerpieces and decorative touches

If you are having your party outdoors, it makes sense to use the landscape as inspiration for table centerpieces.

From the garden, partygivers can take cues from flowers in bloom and seasonal fruits. From the clear blue water of a pool or pond, think fish or things that float.

If the azalea bushes are on fire with hot pink blooms, look for contrasting colors on the table to complement them. If your back yard is furnished with rustic twig furniture, consider carrying that theme to the table in miniature.

Heres how:

Place doll-size twig furniture (sold in craft stores) in the center of the table and weave real or silk greenery around the legs.

Line four new, tiny terra cotta pots with heavy-duty Saran wrap and fill with condiments that complement what you are serving. Place the filled pots on a colored doily, surround with greenery, and you have a very functional centerpiece.

Fill small wire baskets with lemons and tie the handle or rim with a bright blue bow.

Float candles in a small, shallow clear bowl of water. (Party, craft and candle stores sell these.)

Turn a small doll's or child's straw hat upside down and fill with fresh flowers or fragrant tropical fruit.

Use a cluster of small, brightly colored gift bags placed on cut palm fronds or amid grapevines as centerpieces. If you are offering a party gift to your guests, fill the bags and instruct people to take the bags with them when they leave.

Arrange small unpainted pieces intended for papier-mache projects as the focal point of the table. Look for these items in craft stores. Some of the figures available include ducklings, pumpkins and hat boxes. Store offerings change with the seasons. These are inexpensive and light, making them easy to buy and reuse. And even unpainted, they make attractive knickknacks for the table.

Cut fresh flowers from your garden and place in low vases that are tied with coordinating colored ribbon.

Scatter confetti in fun shapes over the tablecloth. Party supply and greeting card stores carry everything from tiny fish to palm trees. If using fish-shaped confetti, set three or four small wood fish (available at import stores) in the center of the table. If using palm trees, set a miniature palm in the center of each table.

Arrange decorative bottles of vinaigrette or salad dressings amid sprigs of the dominant herb used in the recipe. Buy the herbs at supermarkets and garden shops or snip them from your own back yard.

Place small pots of fresh herbs in the center of each table. Just before guests sit down, rub or break a few of the leaves to release a bit their fragrant scent.

Blow up a small (children's-size) pool ring and place it in the center of the table that sits poolside. Fill the center with low plants, toy boats or crisscrossed toy fishing gear.

Greenery salvaged from a shaggy Christmas tree can add color to mantels, coffee tables and a bar. Florists, garden shops and your back yard are sources for decorative greenery as well. Inexpensive gold and silver wire-rimmed bows and ribbons from fabric and craft shops can be fitted around lamp bases and tall candlestick holders for a designer touch.

Some bright ideas

Lighting outdoor dinner parties takes a little know-how, but party planners have many options.

Old-fashioned Oriental lanterns are posh again, and tiki torches have never gone out of style. Those are fine for some parties, but what about sit-down dinners alfresco? Guests do want to see what they're eating.

If you are using a tent, you can do any kind of lighting over the tables. For example, rental companies can provide chandeliers, fancy globes, twinkling lights and color spotlights. But what if the budget or the size of the yard doesn't allow for a rented tent?

Use centerpieces with candles to illuminate place settings. But be careful with citronella-based lights. They emit a black smoke that can soil tablecloths and clothing.

Floating candles (available at party shops) in glass bowls will burn for several hours.

When selecting candles, avoid those with overpowering scents. The fragrance will compete with the aroma of the foods, and some perfumy scents can draw bugs. Also, choose slow-burning, short candles so that dinner guests don't have to bob and weave around the centerpiece to make conversation. Party stores are great sources for these lights, but if you are unsure about what to buy, seek the advice of a specialty candle retailer.

Don't overlook decorative or camping lanterns for shedding light on the table. They lend themselves to just about any casual theme and are especially useful when there is a slight breeze in the air.

Department stores sell battery-operated lights that are designed for campouts but do a swell job of providing light without the hassle of matches and dripping wax. Some are even shaped like small household table lamps. Many partygivers are intrigued with strings of chili pepper, cow, birthday cake and fruit globed lights sold in party shops and through catalogs. While these are fun for table and trellis decorations, don't count on them to light the way for guests.

With the table set and the nuances of lighting dealt with, let's have another round of pina coladas. Your blender or mine?

Invitations

Not only do invitations go directly to the people you want to entertain, they also serve as festive reminders of the party to come for busy friends and family. Whether you shop a stationery store specializing in custom creations or a card shop, look for invitations that give clear information: when, what kind of party (open house, dinner, etc.) and where. The last thing you want to be doing the day of the party is giving directions over the phone to everyone you've invited.

But simple doesn't mean plain. A boring invite may not prompt people to put the date in ink on their calendars. But a personalized note with some pizazz lets people know this will be a gathering they won't want to miss.

When buying invitations, count the number of addresses, not the number of invitees. Sounds simple, but it's an easy and costly mistake to make.

Music

Music is the great mood-setter. It should be upbeat but not overpowering. It should be audible but not at conversation-drowning levels.

And it should be appropriate for the party theme.

The easiest route is to use a seasonal-themed CD recorded by the artist who best suits your crowd. Record stores have special sections for seasonal music. In these bins you'll find everything from Chipmunks and Muppet recordings for children's parties to Elvis Presley, Aaron Neville, Frank Sinatra and Motown for adult get-togethers.

Menu planning tips:

Choose foods that can be partially or fully prepared in advance. You'll appreciate that saving in time and energy on party day. Limit last-minute cooking tasks or reheating to just one or two dishes.

Don't try to do everything yourself. Take advantage of takeout convenience or a catering service. Or, get help in the kitchen. Call on family or friends as co-hosts or helpers.

When ordering foods from specialty markets, gourmet delis, bakeries or restaurants, ask if you can use your own platters and bowls.

Index

Pizza
    brownie banana split 81
    pesto 26

Polenta bites 61

Pork
    Cajun pork roast 52
    rack with parsleyed crumbs 89

Potatoes
    festive hash browns 66
    rosemary 90
    salad 78

Quesadillas, shrimp 25

Raita, cucumber mint 21

Red pepper
    bruschetta with feta 21
    crostini 19
    roasted, onion bread 26

Relish
    artichoke olive 53
    rum mango-cranberry 84

Salads
    artichoke 37
    ceasar 80
    potato salad 78
    roasted Vidalia onions with vinaigrette 72
    spinach citrus salad 64
    tarragon shrimp and orange salad 42
    Texas caviar 18
    triple treat bean salad 50

Salsa
    black bean 20
    tangerine 101

Sandwiches
    beef and honey mustard 50
    muffuletta 45
    Southwest pepperjack 49
    spiral 51
    turkey with artichoke relish 53
    watercress and smoked salmon sandwiches 74

Sauces
    desert flower whiskey sauce 77
    Foster sauce 98

peachy Chinese barbecue 77

Shrimp
    artichoke shrimp casserole 75
    Caribbean shrimp and mushroom packets 44
    Joe's mustard sauce 27
    smoked shrimp and artichoke spread 19
    tarragon shrimp and orange salad 42
    quesadillas 25

Tapenade 22

Tarts
    fruit tarts with citrus curd 75
    quick phyllo pudding 67

Texas caviar 18

Tomato, sun-dried bruschetta with basil 28

Turkey, honey herb-roasted 83

Vegetables
    black-eyed peas 18
    brussels sprouts 84
    garlic, roasted 87